COFFEEHOUSE
CONTEMPLATIVE

Intersections
Theology and the Church in a World Come of Age

Series Editor, Rev. Dr. Christopher Rodkey
St. Paul's United Church of Christ, Dallastown, PA

Advisory Board

Dr. Dan Boscaljon
The University of Iowa, Iowa City, Iowa

Rev. James Ellis, III
Peace Fellowship Church, Washington, DC

Rev. Dr. Kristina Lizardy-Hajbi
*Center for Research, Analytics, and Data,
United Church of Christ, Aurora, CO*

Rev. Bromleigh McCleneghan
Union Church of Hillsdale, United Church of Christ, Hillsdale, IL

Rev. Joshua Patty
Eastgate Presbyterian Church, Independence, MO

Rev. Dr. Robert Saler
Christian Theological Seminary, Indianapolis, IN

Rev. Dr. Phil Snider
Brentwood Christian Church, Springfield, MO

Rev. Dr. John Vest
Union Presbyterian Seminary, Richmond, VA

Introduction to the series

The past century has seen an increased and increasing divide between the guilds of academic theology and the inhabitants and practitioners within the church—especially among American Protestants. So much is this the case that entire seminaries, colleges, and networks of educational institutions exist primarily to shield or suppress the richness of contemporary theology from the church's leadership and its laity. Diminished resources of theological schools and religious publishers have relegated theology and theological reflection to be a luxury for those who splurge in such intellectual desires.

This series from Noesis Press, Intersections: Theology and the Church in a World Come of Age, takes the perspective that theology is not an excess by-product of church practice, but a *necessary* and *foundational* task which fuels and animates the increasingly multifaceted roles of clergy and church leaders in the present. The subtitle of the series is an intentional not to Dieterich Bonhoeffer, whose call for a church in a "world come of age" is to affirm a forward-thinking and self-critical approach to Christianity, even at the expense of Christendom. Of course, Bonhoeffer's contemporary apologists have attempted to galvanize and redefine this to be a clarion call to affirm the past and resist the future.

Bonhoeffer, too, stood at the intersection of the academy and the church. He brought his learned sophistication into the practice of youth ministry and ecumenical dialogue. When the systems of the church and theological schools failed in their mission by affirming the easy triumphalism of nationalism and racism, he led efforts in the confessing church and underground seminary movements. As an intellectual, Bonhoeffer was willing to challenge central theologies of Luther and radically reconsider the relationship of Christ and the church, even pointing toward the possibility of a post-Christendom Christocentrism.

The works presented in this series seek to embody and inhabit these intersections, engaging and inviting church practitioners to think theologically anew, and enticing theologians to return to the ecclesiology, of the contemporary church and its tasks. These works are not presented with a specific confessional or theological bias, but encourage challenging perspectives and introductory texts to concepts and ideas for clergy and laity to envision the future of the Christian faith, whose participants seek to re-connect to the rich intellectual heritage of the church.

This book, *Coffeehouse Contemplative* by Jeff Nelson, fits nicely into one of the goals of this series, which is to accessibly introduce an aspect of practical theology to clergy or laity. Most clergy and well-read laypeople have heard of St. Ignatius of Loyola and what is called "Ignatian Spirituality," but few really explore the depths of it with a spiritual director or receive training in spiritual direction. Some Protestants are skeptical of a spiritual practice so closely aligned with Catholicism, yet Ignatian Spirituality is a religious ethos which transcends denominational entrenchments.

Here we have a simple introduction which takes the theological heavy-lifting very seriously that will be used by clergy and small groups to explore these practices from the guidance of a very able and talented Protestant pastor. Whether you read this book in solitary or with a group, warm your hands around your favorite caffeinated beverage and be prepared to drink deeply.

— Christopher D. Rodkey

Coffeehouse Contemplative
Spiritual Direction for the Everyday

Jeffrey A. Nelson
With a Foreword by John Dorhauer

Noesis Press
Aurora, Colorado

Copyright © 2016 Jeffrey A. Nelson. All rights reserved. No part of this book may be reproduced, stored in an information retrieval system, or transcribed, in any form or by any means—electronic, digital, mechanical, photocopying, recording, or otherwise—without the express written permission of the publisher, and the holder of copyright. Submit all inquiries and requests to the publisher.

Library of Congress Cataloging-in-Publication Data

Names: Nelson, Jeffrey A. author.
Title: Coffeehouse contemplative : spiritual direction for the everyday / Jeffrey A. Nelson ; with a foreword by John Dorhauer.
Description: Aurora, Colorado : Davies Group, Publishers-Noesis Press, 2016.
| Series: Intersections: theology and the church in a world come of age | Includes bibliographical references and index.
Identifiers: LCCN 2016005712 | ISBN 9781934542552 (pbk. : alk. paper)
Subjects: LCSH: Spiritual direction--Christianity. | Spiritual life--Christianity.
Classification: LCC BV5053 .N45 2016 | DDC 248--dc23
LC record available at http://lccn.loc.gov/2016005712

The Scripture quotations contained herein are from the New Revised Standard Version Bible, copyright © 1989 by the Division of Christian Education of the National Council of the Churches in Christ of the U.S.A., and are used with permission. All rights reserved.

Scripture quotations marked (NIV) are taken from the Holy Bible, New International Version®, NIV®. Copyright © 1973, 1978, 1984, 2011 by Biblica, Inc.™ Used by permission of Zondervan. All rights reserved worldwide. www.zondervan.com The "NIV" and "New International Version" are trademarks registered in the United States Patent and Trademark Office by Biblica, Inc.™

For Andrea, Wesley, and Harper

Contents

Foreword by John C. Dorhauer	xii
Acknowledgments	xvi
Chapter 1 — Introduction	1
Companionship for the Journey	3
An Overview of What Follows	7
Questions for Reflection	9
Chapter 2 — Drip Grind Sacrament	11
A Word Needing a Definition	12
On the Road and at the Table: Luke 24	16
It's All Spiritual	21
Questions for Reflection	24
Chapter 3 — A God of Reckless Forgiveness	25
Naming Our Images	26
Jesus, the Image of God	30
Images Influence Awareness	35
Questions for Reflection	37
Chapter 4 — Meeting Ourselves Again	39
The Role of Our Own Experience	40
Breathing Freely	43
Done with False Narratives	47
Questions for Reflection	51
Chapter 5 — Beginning to Listen	53
Quick to Listen, Slow to Speak	54
Using Our Imagination	58
Seeing the Place, Seeing Ourselves	63
Questions for Reflection	66
Chapter 6 — Propane Altars and Dishwasher Shrines	67
Lifting the Veil	72
Coffeehouse Contemplative	76
Questions for Reflection	78

Chapter 7 — Grace in Dry Places	79
Sitting in the Dust	81
Finding Consolation in Desolate Times	84
Desolation in the Psalms	87
Psalms for a New Day	92
Questions for Reflection	94
Chapter 8 — Encountering Together	95
Called into Spiritual Community	97
The Case for Gathering At All	100
The Needs of the Body	103
Questions for Reflection	107
Chapter 9 — Responding to Grace	109
The Possibility of Self	111
Open Eyes, Open Hands	114
Directions on the Road	118
Questions for Reflection	120
Chapter 10 — Immersed in God's Presence	121
A Psalm of Awe	122
Fear, Reverence, and Disorder	126
Immersion, Wisdom, and Awe	128
Questions for Reflection	131
Afterword — Looking Back and Moving Forward	133
Notes	137
Bibliography	143
Index	147

Foreword

My journey into ministry wound through many pathways.

I started out Roman Catholic, and spent eight years in a Diocesan seminary in St. Louis. After meeting and marrying a Lutheran, and years spent in other professions, I felt the call to go back to seminary, this time entering as a Lutheran. Having begun this latest part of my education at a United Church of Christ seminary, my time as a Lutheran would not last, as it was there that I found the church of my heart. I would eventually be ordained in the UCC. Some 15 years later, I would go back to pursue a Doctorate in Ministry through a Methodist seminary.

On that circuitous path to shaping a life in commitment to the gospel, I found a single thread that wove the experience together into a cohesive wholeness: the abiding, brooding presence of the Holy Spirit.

Please don't ask me to explain what I mean by that. Talk of the Holy Spirit, her movement and influence, her unmistakable presence - discernible less through deductive reasoning and more through quiet contemplation - breaks down for me at the level of comprehensive, logical, cogent speech. Words cannot adequately express, nor make sense out of, nor fully communicate what encounters with the Holy Spirit feel like, sound like, look like.

They are in the realm of the ineffable. Efforts to describe such moments are better left to the poets, the artists, the dreamers, the musicians, and the shamans.

I can't say when it was I first experienced a presence that I recognized as beyond me. I know it was well before I had the requisite experience or vocabulary or understanding of the sacred necessary for attaching meaning to it. I do know that it was at a very young age.

Sometimes this experience happened during Mass, when a piece of music would stir the soul or the words of a prayer would touch the heart in a new way. Sometimes it would happen at the river's edge, quiet but for the riffling of shallow waters tumbling incessantly over rock and pebble. Sometimes it was while lying still on a dark night in the deep woods, glimpsing the enormity of the stars in the heavens; or atop some hill or mountain in the stillness of a quiet morning as the sun broke the horizon, the wind touched my cheek, and color transformed night into day.

Sometimes an experience came in long moments of utter but intended silence and solitude; time given to sacred contemplation, disciplined and patient. I would be grateful for the peace that came in such moments and hopeful that some visit from the sacred would offer new insight, new truth, new light.

When I was in the Catholic seminary, prayer and contemplation were structured into our daily lives. We had morning prayer before breakfast, Mass in the midday, evening prayer before dinner, and the vespers late in the evening before retiring to bed. We would break the routine of classwork one day a month with what was called a Day of Recollection. Classes were canceled. One of the priests, or a guest would offer reflections and insights two or three times a day, followed by quiet times of contemplation and prayer. Every year, one week was set aside for a retreat. I would pile into a bus with my classmates and travel to a remote, isolated location and spend that week with them in prayer, conversation, and contemplation.

I had a Spiritual Director each of the eight years I spent at the Catholic seminary. I would meet with her or him once a month. These men and women were trained to test with us how it was with our spirits. It was one thing to know we were doing well with our studies, but in order to form and shape us into an integrated, whole person they helped me pay careful attention to spiritual growth and healing.

Through these experiences, I came to know and understand the power of a variety of spiritual practices, writings, and disciplines.

I learned to meditate. I practiced Lectio Divina. I learned to memorize rote prayers and, rather than roll them off my tongue quickly so as to move on, I learned to take my time; to wait for the sacred to reveal new meaning in a different word or phrase. I learned to journal. I learned to sit quietly in long silences. I read from many spiritual traditions including the Celtic, the mystic, the Sufi, Khabalist, and the Taoist, among others.

Through it all, I went through a spiritual awakening that, when experienced alongside the expansion of my mind while sitting in the classroom, gave me a profound sense of wholeness.

Looking back on those days fills me with a sense of longing. I know now that I was rather sheltered, isolated from the day to day life that most men and women know. My days were structured by others who invested in shaping me into a whole person who would come to see the wisdom in stretching the mind, the heart, the body, the spirit, and the soul.

I am ever so grateful for the foundation that was laid for me in those formative years, but I did not end up choosing to be ordained into the priesthood. Instead, my spiritual pathway would unfold in a very different direction. I would reenter seminary as a Lutheran, and leave it ordained into the United Church of Christ. I would marry and help raise three children while serving as the pastor of two churches, one in a small farm village of 250 people, and the other a small town of about 10,000.

In the twenty-eight years I have spent in ministry, raising a family, and pursuing the enormity of responsibilities that accompany each, the discipline of spiritual rigor that I once knew has been replaced by the demand to meet the daily needs of those I am called to serve.

Outside the shelter and protection of an environment that built spiritual discipline and practice into my daily living, my attention to spiritual disciplines suffered. My days were filled less with time given to prayer and more time given to task. The business of every day crowded out time spent in the pursuit of spiritual wholeness. More than that, however, I learned that without those structures and rigors and disciplines – and someone to build them into your day - there is little that suggests that such practices make any sense at all.

We are all children of Enlightenment thinking. Science and reason and rational thought have made intuition, prayer, and mystery passé. It is truth we are after—the kind of truth that finds encounters with the mysterium and the ineffable nothing more than frustrations that engender deeper commitments to study, experimentation, and theorem.

I feel deeply now the call to reawaken those spiritual longings.

It is not enough to know.

It is not enough to do.

I also must be.

This book by Jeff Nelson is part of my call back to those deep wells of spiritual practices whose waters healed and made me whole. In it he writes: "placing too much stock in words, reason, and intellect have the potential to hinder or devalue our use of silence, imagination, experience, and emotion." He is so right.

Protestant theology and practice are byproducts of Enlightenment thinking. They don't call it a Protestant work ethic for nothing! And training for ministry in the Protestant world engages every brain cell in the pursuit of the deeper knowledge that Enlightenment thinking prized. This came at the expense of the folly of time spent in silence with the sacred.

Jeff concludes this timely book with these words: "When we are fully aware of our immersion in the raw stuff of God's creative activity; our floating in the waves of God's movement, it invites our reverent response. We are called away from our disordered attachments, our destructive images of God and self, and into a new way of engaging the world. This is a proper life of reverence, the psalmist suggests, because it is a life centered on God's awe-inspiring and wondrous deeds. Our thankful response is the beginning of wisdom; the continuation of our spiritual journey."

I agree.

It is time for the mystic within us to emerge.

It is time for the shamans and spiritual directors among us to find our voice. These are men and women whose gift is connection with the sacred, who see things that reveal the movement of God's spirit among us. Jeff is one of them. We would be wise to listen to what their hearts are singing.

— John Dorhauer

Acknowledgments

Writing a book is quite an involved process, and I am grateful to so many people who have given their time, support, feedback, and patience along the way.

I am first glad for Chris Rodkey, my series editor at Noesis, as well as Victor Taylor and James K. Davies of the Davies Group for the opportunity to produce this work, and for your guidance as we moved toward completion.

I spent many afternoons and late nights hunched over a laptop writing and editing, and am glad for the love, understanding, and encouragement of my wife, Andrea, and my children, Wesley and Harper, as I did so.

Thank you to Martha Spong, Sharon Seyfarth Garner, and Chad Abbott for your willingness to read chapters and give suggestions.

Thank you to Dr. Karen Tye, who helped begin this journey at Eden Theological Seminary so many years ago, and to Dr. Joan Nuth and my colleagues and friends at the Ignatian Spirituality Institute for continuing and strengthening it so many years later.

And thank you, dear reader. You're giving this book a chance, and I appreciate that.

Chapter 1

Introduction

Among the many spiritual practices from which one may choose, walking the labyrinth has become especially meaningful for me over the years. For the unfamiliar, this practice involves prayerfully walking a winding path until one reaches the middle of the design, where one is invited to linger as long as they like before walking the same path the opposite direction back through where they entered. Like any practice, labyrinths involve a great amount of mindfulness and openness to what one might receive from doing it.

I have not always done well with this practice, because at times I've attempted to force something, some result, from it. I enter the path with particular questions that I hope to have resolved, and try too hard to make something happen. Needless to say, when I approach it in this way, I leave disappointed. This is, I believe, because sometimes I like the idea of the labyrinth more than actually walking it. It is one thing for me to enjoy the thought of a spiritual practice, but it is quite another to begin observing it. The former may bring an excited anticipation or an anxious uncertainty. Our expectations of what we are about to do may not line up with actually doing it, because the latter may not bring the desired results for which we had hoped, especially the first few times we attempt them.

Given these expectations and questions, we might be finished attempting a regular spiritual practice before we even begin. We set ourselves up to quit because we view such practices as too lofty for us, or we view ourselves as too unspiritual to bother because whatever results we hope to achieve don't materialize on our timetable. We may ask ourselves whether we're even doing this right, which only compounds our sense of frustration and confirms our notion that spirituality is best left to the professionals.

The idea itself of spiritual devotion as unattainable for the average person is intimidating, and it leads the one making the attempt to approach with a mindset much like the one I describe when walking the labyrinth: we try to will something to happen, overly focused on what we're doing to the point that we prevent ourselves from allowing the exercise to unfold. We're too aware of the mechanics of the path to pay attention to what may arise within us along the way. What's more, if we let go enough to be attentive, we may wonder how to decipher the thoughts and feelings we notice as we walk.

I first heard the words "spiritual direction" at the very beginning of my seminary years, a time that is moving further and further away in my life's rear-view mirror. I opted to take an elective class on spiritual practices, and subsequently I learned about the many, centuries-old traditions which are appreciated and observed today in many corners of the world.

Our professor, a contemplative soul who seemed to embody the spirit of what we were learning, shared with us the positive difference that finding a spiritual director could have both while we were still making our way through classes and after graduation. Such a figure in our lives could help us remain prayerful and centered in the face of whatever pastoral situations awaited us in the years to come.

I credit that period of my life with much personal growth, but also with planting the seeds of interest in spirituality that grew within me for years afterward. Along with this early class came regular opportunities to walk a labyrinth, as well as to be encouraged by a weekly meditation group that met on campus. Occasionally, and especially as the completion of my studies neared, teachers and mentors repeated their encouragement to seek out spiritual direction. My response was always to tuck away that piece of advice, like so much else, with the good intentions to revisit it when the time felt right.

Some seven years into my first pastoral position, my good intentions became something more as I enrolled in a program to become certified as a spiritual director. I had not yet pursued the advice of those who advocated retaining such a figure in my life, but here I was planning to become one—those seeds from earlier years beginning to take root, the soil finally tender and tilled enough for something to sprout through.

During my initial interview, however, the program director encouraged me to hold off on beginning classwork for a year. She suggested that I journey through the Spiritual Exercises of Ignatius of Loyola—the focus of the program—before learning how to guide others. After so many years of putting off the advice of my seminary community, I had my very first spiritual director who would offer me guidance over a seven-month stretch as I connected Ignatius' meditative themes to my own life, finally making clear to me spiritual direction's transformative potential.

Whenever I have shared news about my participation in these studies with others, their natural first question is always, "What is spiritual direction?" At first, I always stammered my way through an answer, wondering how best to explain what it was that I was planning to do. For better or worse, people already have a general idea of what pastoral ministry is, so that's relatively easy to explain. But the practice of spiritual direction is not nearly as well known, and thus more difficult to describe. It might take me an entire book to do so.

Companionship for the Journey

The very first clarification that I should make is the use of the word "direction." This word may conjure thoughts and images of one giving orders or instructions to another, and thus signify an unequal relationship where one simply does what another says. Particularly as it relates to spirituality and faith, one may already have negative experiences from which to draw upon encountering this term.

Some have suggested alternatives to the use of "direction," among them "companionship," "guidance," or "friendship." People intend these replacements to avoid the suggestion that spiritual direction is based on hierarchy. Indeed, it would be much more accurate to visualize spiritual direction as two people walking alongside each other, the one describing their experience of the path, the other listening and offering insight into both what he or she hears being described, as well as possibilities to continue traveling it. In spiritual direction, one joins another on their faith journey, helping him or her develop their sense of God's presence and activity in their life, offering observations and guidance rather than micromanagement or conformity. Its primary purpose is to help people foster a deeper connection to God according to their own experiences, needs, and story.

At times while walking a path, we aren't sure about the best way to proceed, or we encounter what we perceive to be hindrances to the journey, or we might want to talk more about an experience we had earlier. In moments like these, the direction of another would be beneficial for helping us sort through the factors, feelings, and questions involved. Perhaps we could figure it out by ourselves eventually, but someone else's perspective and wisdom might open us to possibilities we wouldn't have considered if left only to our own discernment.

A common question in response to this description might be, "Don't you already do this as a pastor?" It is possible that a variety of people including clergy or a trusted friend whom you consider spiritually insightful and grounded could fulfill this role. Others may seek out an officially certified spiritual director, who has been through an intensive program that includes theology, technique, and professional ethics for the specific task of guiding others in this way. Still others may rely on groups through which they find spiritual support, whether a church or something less formal. And still others' journeys are much more self-directed, where books and other materials serve as the only guides one believes they need. No matter the specifics, spiritual direction is the giving or receiving of insight that one cannot cull by force of will and intellect alone. We seek other voices when we realize we don't have all the answers ourselves for the questions and curiosities within us.

In the Apostle Paul's letter to the Romans, he describes the activity of God's Spirit in times of prayer, particularly when those prayers are lifted up in anguish and despair. He writes:

> Likewise the Spirit helps us in our weakness; for we do not know how to pray as we ought, but that very Spirit intercedes with sighs too deep for words. And God, who searches the heart, knows what is the mind of the Spirit, because the Spirit intercedes for the saints according to the will of God (Romans 8:26–27).

In just two verses, we read of several things happening at once. First, God's Spirit is active while one prays, interceding alongside us when our ability to name our deepest longing fails us. At times, when seeking God's presence during prayer, a groan might be all that we have. And so Paul suggests that the Spirit offers her own petitions and laments, praying with us when we cannot pray for ourselves. Our companion in prayer says what needs to be said, even when we can't form the words.

And what allows the Spirit to do this? It is because God, who is of one mind with the Spirit, knows the heart of the person praying. God doesn't just know us by the words we speak, but by our innermost and most desperate yearning. God is that intimately connected with us, even if God might seem elusive in times of darkness and pain.

Henri Nouwen writes, "The goal of spiritual direction is spiritual formation—the ever-increasing capacity to live a spiritual life from the heart. A spiritual life cannot be formed without discipline, practice, and accountability."[1] Developing one's spiritual life takes a great deal of patience and nurturing. The idea of it may be mysterious, romantic, strange, or daunting, but once we actually engage in it, we may find that it is both much more accessible and ordinary than we thought. Spiritual direction may not often bring a sudden new enlightenment, but it will till the soil of our hearts to bring growth over time. It does so by clarifying the connection between our spirituality and the rest of our lives, resulting in a greater recognition that God is with us in the tasks, decisions, and relationships that make up our days rather than apart from them on some mystical, detached plane reachable only by special invocation.

Elsewhere, Nouwen writes:

> The unfathomable mystery of God is that God is a Lover who wants to be loved. The one who created us is waiting for our response to the love that gave us our being. God not only says: "You are my Beloved." God also asks: "Do you love me?" and offers us countless chances to say "Yes." That is the spiritual life: the chance to say "Yes" to our inner truth.[2]

One assumption behind spiritual direction is that God is already in relationship with us, and we have the capacity to discern that relationship; to respond to God's loving invitation that has been with us our whole lives. Like any other relationship, this involves conscious and careful tending in order for it to thrive. God's love for us can be more than an idea. It can be an act of intentional response to this divine affirmation by pondering its meaning and purpose.

When we don't know how to pray or how to identify God's connection with us, our greatest ally may be a guide to give name to our experiences for which we might not yet have the vocabulary. When we are fumbling along the path, wondering where God has been and how to describe what we most yearn for, we may need another to pray with us; to help find the right words, to offer wisdom regarding how to quiet our hearts enough in order to find God there.

That is spiritual direction—a process of helping another deepen his or her awareness of God; to help water the seed of divine providence already planted within. Such a journey will greatly benefit from a companion to pray for and with a traveler prone to wonder where it's all going.

An Overview of What Follows

Several purposes interweave at the root of this book. First, you will be introduced to the practice of spiritual direction, and how it might aid in your own journey. Second, each of the following chapters examines a theme that may arise in spiritual direction in whatever form it may take for you. Finally, this book is meant to be a spiritual direction resource itself, inviting you to consider how these topics manifest in your own life.

This book is for the spiritually curious and the well-seasoned. It is for those who have devoted themselves to the church, those with one foot out the door wondering if there's anything more, and those who only darken the sanctuary threshold for weddings and funerals. It is for those who wonder about the word "spirituality" itself, how it may be defined, and whether its use is worthwhile.

We will begin at this last point. The next chapter will explore the term "spirituality:" its increased popularity and general use in a shifting cultural landscape, as well as some of the assumptions about it.

Chapters 3 and 4 will invite reflection on the two principle figures involved in one's personal spirituality: God and self. In the former, you will be encouraged to name how you conceptualize God and how the images with which you are most familiar inform your spiritual life, including your sense of self. This will lead to a treatment of other factors that may influence how we view and conduct ourselves, as well as how giving greater care and attention to our spirituality may liberate our true selves from the false fronts we convey to others.

Chapter 5 will explore prayer, and encourage the development of one's capacity to listen to God as well as speak. This will introduce the concepts and practices of meditation and contemplation, and how they may aid in this exercise. Chapter 6 will build upon these definitions in presenting ways to discern God's presence in all our daily tasks, from the simple and routine to the unusual and extraordinary.

Chapter 7 will take a bit of a dark turn by raising the question of how to perceive God in times of spiritual despair. This topic surely does not come with a simple solution, but the right spiritual tools and support around us can at least ease our search through the wilderness.

We continue with the topic of having support around us in chapter 8, which deals with the importance of being in spiritual community. Whether this is a handful of trusted confidants and guides or a larger traditional congregation, we are not meant to journey alone.

Chapters 9 and 10 will provide reflection on the long-term effect that intentional spiritual nurture is meant to have on our outlook on and interaction with the world. Through giving careful attention to our spiritual needs, we begin to consider the spiritual dimension in all of life, and engage it more thoughtfully and prayerfully.

This will by no means be an exhaustive look into spirituality in general or spiritual direction in particular. However, it will at least provide an overview of what you may encounter when you choose to cultivate this aspect of your life with intentionality. Seeking spiritual direction will have an inevitable ripple effect: as we give greater attention to this piece of ourselves, it changes our perception of both God's place in the reality we know, as well as our own.

Questions for reflection

1. How familiar are you with the terms "spirituality" and "spiritual direction?" What are your assumptions about each, and what do you hope to learn about each in the chapters ahead?

2. How would you describe your spiritual path today? What possibilities, roadblocks, or crossroads are you currently facing? How are you currently receiving guidance from others as you navigate the way ahead?

3. Write down a list of current spiritual questions you are considering as you begin this book. Keep that list close by over the course of your reading. Pray over them at the conclusion of each chapter, offering them to God as you reflect on what you have read. Consider how points of clarity or even more questions arise, and to whom you could turn to help you process them further.

Chapter 2

Drip Grind Sacrament

She walked into my office wearing a nervous smile. We were meeting for the first time to begin an eight-week version of Ignatius of Loyola's *Spiritual Exercises,* a shortened overview of the full retreat that would include daily prayer and reflection on scripture passages, as well as a few other meditations. We'd meet weekly to talk about her experience, and I would offer tips and guidance on themes and practices for the new week.

As she sat on the couch across from me, she voiced her hesitation regarding what she was about to do. "I'm really going out of my comfort zone for this," she explained. "I don't know what to expect or how this will go. My mom thinks I'm crazy for doing it! She told me, 'I'm glad you are, because I sure wouldn't!'"

As the weeks progressed, this hesitation faded. Most meetings featured an account of her ability to enter imaginatively into the scripture stories suggested to her. She noted a more peaceable engagement with difficult situations at her job. And with joy and amazement, she described her awareness of a presence with her; a consciousness that she wasn't alone in her daily interactions. Over eight weeks of prayerful study, she'd begun cultivating a new way of seeing the world; of seeking the divine undertones to each interaction and experience of her day.

In truth, this experience had less to do with me and more to do with her own willingness to enter into an intentional time of spiritual direction. I had made an open invitation to people in my congregation interested in making such a retreat, but it was her own hunger and curiosity that had inspired her to take up this discipline. A venture out of her comfort zone had revealed to her a new frontier of spiritual exploration.

A Word Needing a Definition

In my own denomination, the United Church of Christ, as well as many similar denominations and traditions, the hesitation expressed by my directee is quite common. Many who participate in mainline Protestant church settings may feel uncomfortable with the word "spirituality," let alone the concept. Spiritual practices as many know them are seldom explored aside from the content of the Sunday morning worship moment, which may typically feature corporately read and responsive prayers, a standard selection of familiar and beloved songs, a few scripture readings, and a time to listen to a sermon. If one serves on a ministry group or attends another function during the week, there may be a prayer to bless the proceedings in some arbitrary fashion.

For many, this compartmentalization of spiritual practices is enough. It serves them well their entire lives, and has for generations: worshippers feel a certain connection to those who preceded them and, if done well, a certain reverence. What has become known as "traditional" worship communicates a sacred time; an hour or more truly set aside that looks and sounds little like the workplace, the morning commute, the YMCA, and wherever else one may find oneself the rest of the week. This is a solemn time to think, sing, and talk about God. For many, it even embodies something about how we're meant to approach God: organizers and attendees alike intend it to be excellent, well-crafted, respectful, and taken seriously. In such a context, many frown upon audible or visible distractions such as noisy children, coffee cups in the sanctuary, or someone not dressing to an unspoken standard. These disruptions deviate from the script; they don't respect the sense of God's presence that this time set apart means to convey.

Mainline Protestant churches love words: they love writing, saying, hearing, and thinking about words. As such, our worship has plenty of words, carefully considered and selected and spoken.

We value their meaning and know how powerful they can be when chosen either well or poorly. Many of our traditions have produced beautiful prayers, theologically rich hymns, and convicting sermons over many decades. In the context of a Bible study, we discuss the words of scripture, both what they meant in their own context and how they might relate to our own. In placing such a high value on words, we also value the intellect; the mind's capacity to consider God's nature and how best to carry out what we discern to be God's mission for us.

Attention to respectful order and rigorous intellectual development is a wonderful trait for churches and individual believers to have. A Sunday morning worship time that flows well and holds its participants to a higher standard can help nurture a sense of God who also holds us to a higher standard; who calls us to a life set apart from our wider culture's values that often conflict with what God asks of us. Words can be beautiful and poetic and informative, and God having blessed us with the gift of reason is a pretty clear indication that God wants us to use it when considering matters of faith, theology, morality, ethics, and societal concerns.

As we consider the meaning and practice of spirituality, placing too much emphasis on these things can lead to some blind spots. First, such a heavy focus on Sunday morning worship as the primary expression of spiritual practice often means that one will experience an incredibly small percentage of possibilities available to Christian believers, especially in a culture becoming more diverse, ecumenical, and post-denominational. For instance, most UCC churches of which I've been a part are based in the Reformed tradition, which is inspired by the theology and liturgical instruction of Ulrich Zwingli and John Calvin. The structure of worship that comes from this tradition is fourfold: gathering, confession and assurance, hearing the Word, and responding to the Word.[1] Many find this approach meaningful to their experience of God and of spiritual community, but it is one strand of tradition as practiced by churches in a particular cultural setting. If I only insisted on this one expression to the exclusion of others, I would miss out on a thick, rich, vast, and beautiful tapestry of belief and practice that could inform my awareness of God's presence and activity so much more than any single thread alone.

Second, while it is important to respect both the space and time of the weekly worship moment, holding a particular room and hour as sacred detracts from the ways other times and places can be sacred as well. We end up discounting the times when we may be able to discern God's presence while we happen to be wearing blue jeans, nursing a cup of coffee, or interacting with an active, talkative child.

Finally, placing too much stock in words, reason, and intellect have the potential to hinder or devalue our use of silence, imagination, experience, and emotion. Many are prone to see these sorts of elements in spiritual practice as too "Jesus and me;" overly individualistic and based on faulty, non-objective criteria.[2] Thus, many reject such practices because they seem too unreliable or fanciful, bringing discomfort or suspicion. This mindset tends to discourage or avoid language of an experiential relationship with God, instead placing high priority on intellectual discernment of who God is and what God asks of us. This results in many dedicated churchgoers, among others, casting the concept of "spirituality" in a negative light, causing the sort of hesitation displayed by my directee.

On the other hand, the United States is experiencing a growing interest in spirituality. The first part of the 21st century has seen the rise of a belief identity known as "spiritual but not religious." Attempts to define what this category encompasses have brought difficulty, but we can make several generalities. Those who claim this term carry a reputation among some as using it to avoid any serious consideration of religious experience or a longer conversation about specific belief claims. While that may be true of a certain percentage, my concern here are those within this designation who are actively living into its meaning.

Those who are "spiritual but not religious" believe in a transcendent of some sort; some larger reality to which we are connected. Some in this category may call this transcendent "God," but others may know it by other names such as a Higher Power, nature, or the universe. The specifics of the scope and definition may vary greatly, and the trappings of church structures, creeds, and expressions in seeking to define or experience it have left this group unsatisfied. They may see traditional church practices as too confining or too rigid in scope; they may crave more freedom to explore and express such belief that a highly word- and intellect-based environment doesn't allow.

What isn't clear are the kinds of beliefs and practices pursued by those claiming this identity. Some walk a more independent path of self-study and exploration, while others pursue group practices such as drumming circles or yoga classes. Some may find meaning by participation in artistic expressions such as painting, dance, or music. But "spiritual but not religious" people will uniformly stay away from any religious institution that by their perception has the potential to limit their experience, hence the latter part of the term.[3]

Much needs to be clarified regarding how this categorical group uses the words "spiritual" and "spirituality": in many ways the use of these words are employed in a way that defies clarification. At the very least, they may be used to denote a belief in God with a rejection of any formal religious expression. There may or may not be any intentional individual or group practice meant to deepen a connection with God involved. All the same, one gift that those who seriously pursue this identity offer to those still involved with traditional religious expressions and institutions is that an experience of God is possible in many ways and places beyond the walls of one's house of worship.

Whereas "spiritual" may evoke suspicion from some who treasure church participation, it may be a word still in search of a definition by those who have given up such involvement but still seek a connection to something beyond themselves. Serious consideration of the concept and practice of spirituality has more to offer both groups than perhaps either realizes.

On the Road and at the Table: Luke 24

This is a book specifically about Christian spirituality. As such, most of the definitions, concepts, and practices will be grounded in the scriptures used by the Christian faith and in the person of Jesus Christ. As we begin to consider a definition of spirituality that will carry us through the rest of these pages, we will first spend some time with a story from Luke 24 of two disciples walking to the town of Emmaus on the same day that Jesus was resurrected:

Now on that same day two of them were going to a village called Emmaus, about seven miles from Jerusalem, and talking with each other about all these things that had happened. While they were talking and discussing, Jesus himself came near and went with them, but their eyes were kept from recognizing him. And he said to them, "What are you discussing with each other while you walk along?" They stood still, looking sad. Then one of them, whose name was Cleopas, answered him, "Are you the only stranger in Jerusalem who does not know the things that have taken place there in these days?" He asked them, "What things?" They replied, "The things about Jesus of Nazareth, who was a prophet mighty in deed and word before God and all the people, and how our chief priests and leaders handed him over to be condemned to death and crucified him. But we had hoped that he was the one to redeem Israel. Yes, and besides all this, it is now the third day since these things took place. Moreover, some women of our group astounded us. They were at the tomb early this morning, and when they did not find his body there, they came back and told us that they had indeed seen a vision of angels who said that he was alive. Some of those who were with us went to the tomb and found it just as the women had said; but they did not see him." Then he said to them, "Oh, how foolish you are, and how slow of heart to believe all that the prophets have declared! Was it not necessary that the Messiah should suffer these things and then enter into his glory?" Then beginning with Moses and all the prophets, he interpreted to them the things about himself in all the scriptures.

As they came near the village to which they were going, he walked ahead as if he were going on. But they urged him strongly, saying, "Stay with us, because it is almost evening and the day is now nearly over." So he went in to stay with them. When he was at the table with them, he took bread, blessed and broke it, and gave it to them. Then their eyes were opened, and they recognized him; and he vanished from their sight. They said to each other, "Were not our hearts burning within us while he was talking to us on the road, while he was opening the scriptures to us?" That same hour they got up and returned to Jerusalem; and they found the eleven and their companions gathered together. They were saying, "The Lord has risen indeed, and he has appeared to Simon!" Then they told what had happened on the road, and how he had been made known to them in the breaking of the bread. (Luke 24:13–35 NRSV)

During these disciples' journey, they are joined by a figure unfamiliar to them, although the narrator of the story lets the reader know that it is the risen Jesus. Rather innocently, he asks his fellow travelers what they are discussing as they walk. One of the two, Cleopas, recounts in brief the events of the past few days: Jesus showing himself to be a prophetic figure who displayed God's power, and his subsequent arrest, condemnation, and death. He intimates that he and many others had such high hopes for what Jesus would do, but now, for him and many others, that hope is lost.

There is a second part to Cleopas' report, however. He tells of some women from their group who had shared news of an empty tomb and a vision of the risen Jesus. In response, others traveled to the tomb to verify this, but found nothing. When it is Cleopas' new companion's turn to speak, he chastises them for not understanding what has happened that has been foretold in the scriptures. The rest of their walk involves Jesus interpreting these scriptures to them.

The trio finally reaches their destination, and Jesus acts as if he will continue on his way. The disciples insist that he join them for the night, and so they sit down to eat together. While they are seated at the table, Jesus breaks bread and gives it to them; in this familiar act, they realize the identity of this stranger who has been with them for most of the day. Jesus, newly resurrected, has journeyed with them during their conversation on the road and now in their place of lodging, including at this shared meal. They finally are able to recognize him because they've seen him perform this act of taking bread, giving thanks, and giving it to others. They've seen him do it in the feeding of over 5000 people on a hillside in order to satisfy their hunger, and perhaps more fresh in their minds is his sharing the Passover meal with them just before his death. The writer of Luke also intentionally evokes the Eucharistic meal in this moment. While Jesus is not sharing communion with the disciples here, this episode's allusion to both past stories and future observances helps illustrate that any instance of hospitality or fellowship over a meal can be sacred.[4]

This realization is enough to give Cleopas and his friend pause to reflect on the earlier events of the day: "were not our hearts burning within us as while he was talking to us on the road, while he was opening the scriptures to us?" (Luke 24:32) Even then, while they weren't able to name what they were feeling, they had some sense that something was different, beyond the presence of an additional acquaintance. Something had been stirring within them, but at the time they weren't able to identify its cause or meaning. Now, in hindsight, it is more clear to them that their walk together was a sacred time as well; that Jesus had been with them even when they couldn't discern it.

The Protestant tradition lifts up two rituals of the church as sacraments: baptism and communion. They feature ordinary objects and actions that help communicate the presence of God in a particular way. We sprinkle or immerse in water to celebrate the activity of God in the life of a person either new to the world or new to the faith, and pray with them that they will come to know and accept that presence with deeper understanding, gratitude, and commitment.

Likewise, we re-enact Jesus' final meal with his disciples through bread and cup, at times recalling the clarity such a reenactment provided for the two disciples traveling to Emmaus. We not only remember Jesus' original sharing of these elements, but re-member ourselves as part of the community called to bear witness to the risen Christ's continuing presence in the church and in the world, just as the two disciples rushed back to their companions to proclaim, "It is true! The Lord has risen!"

In my own tradition's theological language, we call these sacraments outward signs of God's invisible grace. We use water, bread, and cup—objects we can see and feel and taste—to point out a reality that we can't always sense in or around us. When officiating at the communion table, I raise these tangible items and say, "These are the gifts of God for the people of God," not meaning that God gives us the bread and wine so much as the ways in which we experience God's intangible gifts through them. They are visible gifts communicating invisible grace.

And what is the nature of this grace? Theologian Karl Rahner explains it in this way: "Grace is God himself, the communication in which he gives himself to man as the divinizing favour which he is himself."[5] In other words, the gift of grace that we celebrate particularly in the sacraments is God's very presence, an invisible and freely given gift of love made newly visible every time we watch or partake of these two acts. When we participate in baptism and communion, we are consciously participating in God's presence itself.

And yet Rahner is quick to clarify, it is not only in these actions through which we may receive this gift. God is always giving this grace, even outside the church and its formal customs. In fact, he argues, grace is not even confined to a moment of conscious choice on the part of the receiver. Rather, we are always participating in the gift of God's presence whether or not we are reflecting on how it is so. Moments like the sacraments provide opportunities to remember and renew our participation, but the reality of grace is true even when we aren't actively contemplating it.[6]

The nature of this gift is more than communicated truth. It is rooted in a God who chooses to be in close proximity with us. God's presence is personal to each creature; God is in relationship to us intimately rather than objectively, yet this relationship is most fully actualized when we become aware of it and respond to it.[7] The sacraments, among so many other elements and events that we encounter each day, invite this response if we are tapped in to the gift to which it points.

The disciples in Luke 24 are unaware of the risen Christ walking with them until they sit down together to share a meal. While receiving bread at the table is not the sacrament per se, it nevertheless becomes sacramental, causing them to recognize Jesus for the first time on their journey. But they are also able to reflect back on the day and see how the gift of the risen Christ's presence had been with them all along, stirring their spirits even when they didn't know that it was so.

Not every moment is a sacrament, but every moment has the potential to be sacramental. God is always offering us the gift of God's own presence, a grace that is always with us. At times it may take the specific rituals and elements recognized by the church to help us name what we've been given. At other times, it may be a walk on the road or dining with friends to bring this truth into active consciousness. It is not only water, bread, and cup that help us remember and re-member, but hundreds of other acts and objects every day hold the capacity to help us name what is burning in our hearts.

It's All Spiritual

When my family sits down to eat dinner, my son is very particular about the position of the food on his plate. He has a standing decree that each element making up the meal on any given evening must not touch any other at any time. He sets up invisible barriers that each must not cross, lest an incident erupt that echoes throughout the house. I look upon his insistence with some understanding, as I erected my own food boundaries when I was his age: the macaroni and cheese was evermore to be separate from the green beans, and neither was to come in contact with the chicken. If my son now, or my younger self then, was ever asked to explain why our dining experience had to be this way, I'm not sure that either of us could really venture much of an explanation other than that's how we prefer it to be.

We face the same tendency and temptation to section off parts of our lives, one from another. Some of this is in the name of observing healthy boundaries as we attempt to avoid bringing work-related issues home, lest they encroach on our time spent with family or otherwise in leisure. Likewise, we may not wish to bring personal issues to the workplace, as they may infringe on our ability to do our job well. Some crossover is inevitable, such as considering how a decision at one will affect the other. In general, however, we tend to consider the best approach in most cases to keep these items separate on our plate, for reasons that make more sense than mere habit or preference.

In the case of spirituality, such a practice may be more complicated. In public, communal, and civic situations, the case has been made often for why one's personal spiritual beliefs, or the beliefs of one group, should not be privileged over others. On occasions past and present, doing otherwise has lessened the standing, contributions, and at times the humanity of those whose beliefs (or non-beliefs) differ from the person or group enjoying special treatment. In this way, an argument for compartmentalization of one's plate makes sense and may benefit from encouragement.

At a personal level, the erecting of boundaries between one's own spirituality and the rest of one's life may be detrimental. Some may content themselves to have that one sacred hour on Sunday serve as the extent of one's spiritual life, the tiny God-box in the corner of the soul that gets opened once a week and on special occasions. Spirituality is for the entire self, for our lives of work and family, of business and play. The gift of God's presence graces all of it, meant to affect everything else on our plate even if we prefer that other parts remain separate.

We have spent this first chapter exploring some ways people conceive spirituality, yet have not ventured a concise working definition. Here, finally, one is presented: spirituality is our sense of connection to something larger than ourselves (namely, for Christians, God as revealed in Jesus), and also our sense of self as a participant in that larger reality. If we give it proper attention and space to grow, it may expand into every other part of our identity; all else that makes up who we are and how we view the world.

The possibilities for such meaning-making are all around us, encompassing everything on our plate. Everything has the potential to be sacramental; to help point us toward God's presence around us and within us, as well as help point to who we are and meant to be as recipients of and participants in it. Rather than for a sacred time and place set apart, spirituality most thrives when it transcends the boundaries that we attempt to set around it.

To consider what this looks like, imagine standing in line at a coffeehouse, waiting to place your order. People are behind you and in front of you, awaiting the same opportunity. The man behind you is noticeably agitated, occasionally letting out an exaggerated audible sigh while glancing at his watch. You may take note of your own reaction to him, and how your possible feelings of irritation affect your relationship to God and to your fellow patron. It may also be that you feel convicted by what may be causing anxiety in his life that goes beyond a long wait for coffee.

You get to the front of the line, where you encounter the barista, a young woman who after taking your order appears to be fighting back tears as she turns away to begin preparing it. You caught hints of this from further back in line, but now can see more clearly that this is what has been happening. You may take a moment to wonder who is loving her through whatever difficulty she is facing.

After receiving your order, you sit down at a nearby table. A group of teenagers sit near you obviously enjoying their time together, their laughter and jokes at times filling the room. You may take a moment to consider God's presence in enjoyment shared in community, and even give thanks for similar groups of which you are a part.

You notice an older gentleman in ragged clothing in the corner nursing his own coffee. You may wonder how he got here and where he is going; who might serve as God's representative to him through acts of kindness or more regular social services. At another table, a mother and two young children silently share deli sandwiches, the woman in particular with a strained nervousness behind her eyes. What are these people's stories, and how is God a part of each, consciously or otherwise?

For every person whom you see or hear in this place, for every interaction and encounter, there comes the opportunity to consider how God's gift of grace is a part of the moment, whether every participant is aware of it or not. And this is but one series of such experiences that takes place in the span of an hour, far removed from the usual hourly worship experience either treasured weekly or rejected long ago. Nurturing our spirituality makes it possible for a coffeehouse to become a sanctuary and other patrons our fellow contemplative pilgrims. If our awareness of our participation in God's presence may be deepened with something so ordinary as a cup of coffee, how much more might be possible on the other sections of your plate?

Questions for Reflection

1. What comes to mind when you hear the words "spiritual" or "spirituality?" How do you tend to define it?

2. Do you consider yourself a dedicated member of a faith tradition or institution, or do you identify more as "spiritual but not religious?" How do you think the two may overlap or could learn from the other?

3. Can you name particular moments or practices in your life that you would consider sacramental? It could be a memory of a certain event, or an ongoing meaningful activity. How has what you name deepened your sense of God's presence?

4. How would you say your current spirituality influences other parts of your life, whether your work, family, hobbies, or sense of self? How would you like to improve such influence?

Chapter 3

A God of Reckless Forgiveness

As a spiritual director, a common question that I ask when meeting with a potential directee for the first time is "Who is God for you?" The intent is to get a sense of how the person conceptualizes God, whether through what he or she has been taught by religious communities or through one's own personal study and experience. The answer reveals some of the images of God that are most—and in some cases, least—helpful for making sense of who God is and how God works for that person.

God is the first of two agents involved in any contemplative exercise, the one with whom the person praying desires closer relationship. As such, it is worthwhile to consider the image of God one has in mind while seeking such an encounter. What are the character traits, attributes, demeanor, and intentions of the divine person or presence to whom we wish to draw nearer? The question, "Who is God for you?" invites us to name who and what we have in mind.

When I call an old college friend to catch up, I have a set of ideas about him before the conversation begins. I remember what he looks like from the last time we saw each other and from more recent pictures of him on social media. I have memories of past interactions and moments that shaped our friendship into what it is. I can recall stories he has told from the last time we talked and have a general idea of his career plans and family life. I know his personality; his likes and dislikes. I carry all of this into my latest correspondence whether I'm aware of it or not. This image of who I know my friend to be provides a framework for what I say, how I say it, and my hopes for the outcome of the call, which is usually continued or deepened relationship with him.

Likewise, we carry an image of God into a new moment of encounter, whether in prayer, worship, Bible study, or a myriad of other possibilities. We have a set of ideas about who God is and what God is like, and they shape what we might give the most attention in any spiritual practice. Our answer to "Who is God for you?" names our image of who we know our partner in the divine encounter to be. Who we believe we are addressing shapes our method of address.

Naming Our Images

When I was 12 years old, I had a dream about Jesus. It was the only time that I can ever recall having such a dream, and I have always been curious why I have never had another. This dream was not particularly long, but the interaction is memorable even after so many years.

In this dream, Jesus is sitting at my grandparents' dining room table. A large group of children swarm around him, and he takes them, one by one, on his lap and has a brief conversation with each. After a few such interactions, the crowd parts to allow my approach. He looks at me with a smile and says, "Jeff . . . there is so much on your mind." The dream ends a moment later.

To provide a little more context, this dream took place around the time that my father, a pastor, had encountered a difficult experience at the church he was serving in those days, which had put an emotional strain on my entire family. We were facing the possibility of my father and the church parting ways, as well as a move to a new community. Not only had the conflict with members of the congregation left an impression on me, but I was also about to weather the trials of junior high school, which is difficult enough without having to start over in a new district.

Jesus' physical appearance in this dream is also worth a comment. In those years, the two primary artistic depictions of Jesus with which I was familiar were a popular portrait by Warner

Sallman entitled "Head of Christ" and Robert Powell's portrayal in the Franco Zeffirelli film *Jesus of Nazareth*. I have no doubt that these influenced the image conjured by my subconscious: light-skinned with long brown hair and a beard to match. And yet he also had a familiarity about him in a more intangible way that I wouldn't notice until reflecting later: there were hints of my father in his appearance and mannerisms, most notable in the way he spoke assuredly to me.

This image of Jesus invites critique and evaluation from multiple angles, particularly the certainty that he would have had a much darker complexion during his earthly life given the region in which he lived and traveled. One could also analyze the traits of my father woven into this image and their possible meaning. The Jesus I met in my dream was an amalgam of these representations.

Even so, for a pre-adolescent boy with questions related to his family, life in the church, and his future, a Jesus with familiar traits acknowledging that uncertainty was a helpful image. My understanding of Jesus; the images of him to which I would be drawn and in which I would find meaning have changed over time, but at least for that moment it provided comfort and reassurance. Thus, I would name this image as having a positive effect when I needed it.

There are two general traditions regarding how we are able to speak about or relate to God. The first is the apophatic tradition, which is sometimes called the *via negativa*. This theological strand argues that because human language is so limited, we are unable to really describe God to any satisfactory degree. God is beyond such language, and any attempt to the contrary runs the risk of reducing God to humanity's level, or raising any particular image to God's level.[1] Scholars trace this tradition back to the beginnings of eastern Christianity, which has long emphasized God's unknowable and mysterious nature. Early Christian thinkers such as Gregory of Nyssa resisted the use of icons in worship and personal devotion.

Applied to my dream above, the apophatic tradition would cite the many limitations of the image of Jesus that I encountered: it was based on flawed depictions from other media that are not historically accurate, and it was influenced by the appearance and behavior of at least one person with whom I am acquainted. As God is so radically different from any creature—including those who in any way contributed to the image of Jesus in my dream—it is better to know God in terms of what God is not.[2]

The apophatic tradition can be helpful in at least two ways. First, as illustrated above, it provides a counterpoint to the images of God that we use by pointing out their imperfections and serving as a reminder that no image or set of images may fully encapsulate the vast and incomprehensible nature of God. Harvey Egan states it thus: "[the apophatic tradition] underscores in an unusually powerful way that the human heart is satisfied by nothing other than God. It points to the ever-greater God, a God greater than our hearts, the Ineffable, the Nameless, utter Mystery, who can be loved because He has first loved us."[3]

The apophatic tradition also gives permission to name and dismiss images of God that are unhelpful or destructive. Belief in a God who is primarily punitive and angry, for instance, results in the believer living in constant spiritual anxiety of committing the smallest mistake for fear of how this God might respond. Spiritual director William Barry describes a conversation with a man with such a belief, during which he asks the man, "Do you like this God?" and he quickly responds, "No, I hate him."[4] For this man, this image of God caused a deep resentment rather than stimulated a life of loving discipleship. The apophatic tradition shows us that we are free to reject such images as being neither true nor inspiring truth.

The second tradition concerning how one may speak of or relate to God is the kataphatic,[5] sometimes called the *via affirmativa*. This strand argues that one is able to find God in everything, and encourages the use of images and symbols as ways to describe what God is like. This tradition emphasizes God's self-revelation in creation, scripture, history, and the person of Jesus, and states that such revelations are still possible, helpful, and necessary for theological language and spiritual practice today.[6] Applied to my dream, the kataphatic tradition might say that, while perhaps not a fully accurate depiction of Jesus, it nevertheless served its purpose for a particular time and situation, bringing comfort and assurance to a young boy who needed it. The symbol, while imperfect, nevertheless contained that to which it pointed,[7] and aided one's experience of the divine. God has incarnated in Christ and self-revealed in creation and symbol before, and the image encountered in this dream ultimately points beyond itself; that to which it points is the main concern.

The kataphatic tradition recognizes the limits of language and symbol, but nevertheless encourages their use to make sense of something beyond our knowing. It allows us to make even the most basic positive statements about God, such as "God exists," "God created," or "God is wise."[8] Furthermore, Kevin O'Brien acknowledges that all people of faith have some image of God with which they work, many of which are derived from scripture such as father, mother, judge, Spirit, or Jesus. At the same time, however, these images evolve over time according to our experience and what we find meaningful in new circumstances.[9] As with the man who stated his hatred for a vengeful God above, images that serve more as a barrier to a sense of relationship with God should be named as such, while new ones take their place.

When we approach any spiritual practice, we operate under a set of assumptions about the One whom we are seeking. We have some image of our conversation partner in mind, and this in turn affects what we seek and how we seek it. Naming our images is worthwhile in order to consider whether or how they are true to the believer's experience, edifying to the deepening of the divine/human relationship, and instructive for any spiritual exercise.

Jesus, the Image of God

As the kataphatic tradition invites us to name our images of God, having deemed their use worthwhile when they inspire life, love, and a positive view of the divine, I will now take some time to name some general characteristics of the image of God that will guide the reflections in this book.

For Christians, our primary image of God is in the person of Jesus. In John 14:9, Jesus declares, "Whoever has seen me has seen the Father." That is, to look at Jesus is somehow to see God. Jesus' words, actions, and interactions show us the most complete embodiment of what God is like. The theologian Karl Rahner writes that when we read about God fulfilling the law of loving one's neighbor, it is because God actually became the neighbor.[10] For Christians, Jesus best reveals how God wishes for us to live in the world, because the essence of God is most visibly and completely present in him.

Jesus, it first must be said, was a man of his own time. He was a 1st Century Jew who lived near the Sea of Galilee. He would have been immersed in the culture of his era and location, which included a devotion to the teachings and traditions of early rabbinical Judaism. Even as we read stories of the ways he pushed back or expanded upon these beliefs and customs, this is the world in which he lived and in which accounts of his life—first oral and later written—originated.

All the same, when Christians claim that Jesus was the Incarnation of God, we are saying that we most clearly see God's character in Jesus of Nazareth. A natural consequence of that Incarnation was full interaction and participation in and with humanity. Taking this under proper consideration, what image of God do we see in Jesus?

Rather than attempt an exhaustive survey of the entire New Testament, I have chosen to focus on one story that I think exemplifies the image of God that Jesus presents: the story of the woman who anointed Jesus' feet in Luke 7:36–50:

One of the Pharisees asked Jesus to eat with him, and he went into the Pharisee's house and took his place at the table. And a woman in the city, who was a sinner, having learned that he was eating in the Pharisee's house, brought an alabaster jar of ointment. She stood behind him at his feet, weeping, and began to bathe his feet with her tears and to dry them with her hair. Then she continued kissing his feet and anointing them with the ointment. Now when the Pharisee who had invited him saw it, he said to himself, "If this man were a prophet, he would have known who and what kind of woman this is who is touching him—that she is a sinner." Jesus spoke up and said to him, "Simon, I have something to say to you." "Teacher," he replied, "Speak."

"A certain creditor had two debtors; one owed five hundred denarii, and the other fifty. When they could not pay, he canceled the debts for both of them. Now which of them will love him more?" Simon answered, "I suppose the one for whom he canceled the greater debt." And Jesus said to him, "You have judged rightly." Then turning toward the woman, he said to Simon, "Do you see this woman? I entered your house; you gave me no water for my feet, but she has bathed my feet with her tears and dried them with her hair. You gave me no kiss, but from the time I came in she has not stopped kissing my feet. You did not anoint my head with oil, but she has anointed my feet with ointment. Therefore, I tell you, her sins, which were many, have been forgiven; hence she has shown great love. But the one to whom little is forgiven, loves little." Then he said to her, "Your sins are forgiven."

But those who were at the table with him began to say among themselves, "Who is this who even forgives sins?" And he said to the woman, "Your faith has saved you; go in peace."
(Luke 7:36–50 NRSV)

In this passage, Jesus embodies at least three elements of God's character. A woman barges into this gathering uninvited, scandalizing the host and others present. She most likely was watching the dinner outside along with a crowd of onlookers, as was a common occurrence,[11] and could not contain herself any longer. Luke identifies this woman as sinful, although he does not name her particular sin. For the story's purposes, the greater concern is that many of the other attendees have deemed this intruder unworthy and unwelcome by both social and religious custom.

Jesus, however, allows the woman to proceed with what she wants to do: she bathes his feet with her tears, dries them with her hair, anoints his feet with ointment, and continues touching and kissing his feet. Simon watches this intimate act of affection and adoration in disbelief, becoming convinced that Jesus cannot be who others think he is since he lets this continue for so long.

Sensing what his host is thinking, Jesus tells a brief parable about two people who owe debts to the same creditor. In an incredible act of generosity, the creditor cancels the debts, both of which are sizable. Jesus then asks Simon which of the two newly-forgiven debtors will love the creditor more. Simon, perhaps with a roll of the eyes at the obvious answer, "supposes" it will be the one who needed to pay back the larger amount. In the same way, Jesus says, their uninvited guest has experienced forgiveness, which has led to her act of thankfulness and hospitality. At this point, the guests openly wonder at Jesus' audacity to declare sins forgiven, since this is only something that God can do.

Here is the first divine trait that Jesus exhibits during this brief exchange: Jesus shows forgiveness. Acting contrary to his fellow diners, he first welcomes her to touch and show hospitality to him, and publicly proclaims that she is forgiven in the presence of so many others who would withhold it from her. He makes a declaration reserved for divine authority, well aware that he was dining with those who would have been experts on the subject. If that isn't enough, Jesus disregards social convention by letting the woman touch him at all, which due to her status as an unclean sinner would have rendered him unclean as well.[12]

Jesus engaging the woman in this manner in front of polite company, as it were, not only reveals a God who shows forgiveness, but recklessly so. The patron in the parable removes a heavy burden of debt, losing a significant amount of money and even running the risk of appearing to be a foolish investment manager to his peers. In similar fashion, God shows forgiveness even to people who seem least deserving to those who consider themselves guardians of the proper criteria for such things. Jesus shows us a God whose forgiveness transcends whatever human boundaries we may attempt to erect around it.

This leads to the second aspect of God's character that Jesus reveals. The woman, inspired to act despite cultural restriction, shows Jesus love through her cleaning of and caring for his feet. Jesus interprets this to his host as a gesture of hospitality, which he notes Simon did not show him earlier. An uninvited, unconventional guest is observing a convention that the host neglected.

Jesus also interprets this action as a result of forgiveness. After his parable of the two forgiven debts and subsequent question posed to Simon, Jesus suggests that the woman has also been forgiven. In the context of the parable, the implication is that this woman does not receive forgiveness as a result of what she does; rather, she experienced forgiveness prior to this episode.[13] Perhaps she and Jesus interacted earlier in the day, or her mere observance of him at this meal caused a moment of realization within her. Regardless, in addition to being a sign of hospitality, her gesture is also one of gratitude: "her sins, which were many, have been forgiven; hence she has shown great love" (7:47). This display of love is in response to the forgiveness first shown to her.

William Barry writes that when God reveals our sins and shortcomings to us, God does it in such a way so as to inspire greater faith, hope, and love. We may shed tears of sorrow as we face ourselves, but they also may be tears of love for a God whose love surpasses any selfish or hurtful attitude or behavior on our part.[14] These are the tears with which the woman bathes Jesus' feet: tears of affection and thanksgiving for the forgiveness shown to her. She is, as Barry says, inspired to greater faith, hope, and love.

Thus Jesus reveals a God who transforms us first through reaching out to us in love and forgiveness. God freely and recklessly shares these gifts with us, and once we fully realize and receive them, we are filled with gratitude. This gratitude ignites a change, a desire to move and grow in what we have received.[15] Like the woman who anointed Jesus, we are moved to tears and adoration, but also sent forth in a newfound peace with self and with God to live as thankful recipients of something that doesn't allow us to remain as we were before.

Now we arrive to the final divine characteristic revealed by Jesus in this story—one which encompasses all of those already discussed. Typically this episode would be a usual home gathering in Simon's house: guests seated around a table, eating, drinking, sharing conversation and stories with laughter. In addition to the guests, a crowd of attendants and others gathered in the street to observe the gathering. Among them is Jesus, chewing and swallowing, and digesting—fully present and sharing in the moment. Once the woman enters, she anoints, dries, kisses, and weeps over skin made calloused and dusty by a day of walking. She shows hospitality and affection to a person she can see, hear, and touch, because this same person somehow first showed divine forgiveness to her.

As mentioned earlier in the chapter, Jesus was a man of his time and place. He was not God in the abstract, aloof from those around him. Rather, he touched lepers, dined with people of diverse backgrounds, healed ailments, wept at a friend's tomb, forgave sins, and met the world as it was at a particular moment in history. As Rahner puts it, grace became completely actualized in Jesus,[16] God's presence fully incarnate for the time in which it lived, in the ways it was needed.

Jesus revealed a God who is imminent; immediately present with and for the particulars from moment to moment. He showed that God is ever self-communicating to us in close proximity rather than from afar. The woman who is moved to interrupt the gathering senses this immediate divine presence, and in thanksgiving wishes to touch her cheek to it once again.

This desire is at the heart of any spiritual practice. When we encounter a God who transforms us through first communicating God's love for us, it draws us in and inspires us to seek more, whatever the circumstances.

Images Influence Awareness

There are many useful images for God. If we attempted to count the possibilities, they could number in the thousands. Scripture itself imagines God in numerous and diverse ways including human images of both genders, animals such as a lion or hen, inanimate objects such as a rock or fortress, or intangibles such as wind or breath. Each of these made sense in its own context, whether the author or audience most desired God's tender care, steadfast protection, righteous anger, or life-giving power. These images served a purpose for a particular moment according to need.

In turn, different images of God may be more meaningful to us at certain times of our lives. For a 12-year-old boy, this was an image of Jesus with familiar characteristics appearing in a moment of uncertainty. For others, depending on time, circumstance, and background, according to knowledge and experience, other divine images might speak to us.

Taking stock of the current images that are most meaningful to us also makes a difference in how we're attentive to God's presence and activity in the world. If, for instance, we tend to see God as a judge, ever weighing and passing sentence on our and others' sins, we may be more prone to interpret tragedies such as illness or natural disasters as its consequences. If we tend to see God as a nurturing parent, we may be more attentive to what we perceive as gentle or overt nudging to move out of our comfort zones into new avenues of faithfulness.

As we have considered the image of God revealed through Jesus, I have noted at least three divine attributes that we see exhibited in his life. We see reckless forgiveness that scandalizes even the most religiously devoted people of every era. We see gracious transformation, where this forgiveness inspires us to interact with those around us in a new way. We see an earthy imminence in the world, a presence concerned with the daily lives of God's creatures rather than distant from them.

These characteristics make a difference in our cultivating an awareness of God in the everyday. Considering God's reckless forgiveness in an argument with a coworker or in our struggles with the way we've wronged someone will change the dynamic of how we seek a resolution. Our own reception of this forgiveness in particular will influence and transform how we handle such disputes in the future, as well as inspire a more thankful and selfless way of life. Finally, an image of God who is in close, invested proximity to us is the very cornerstone on which many spiritual practices are built.

In particular, our image of God affects how we see ourselves. This will be our focus in the next chapter.

Questions for Reflection

1. What images of God have been most helpful to you? How have such images changed over time? What images are most meaningful for you at this point in your life?

2. Between the kataphatic or apophatic tradition, which makes more sense to you? How do you think each is valuable for your own consideration of divine images?

3. As you consider the life and ministry of Jesus, what divine characteristics stand out to you the most? How does reflecting on the stories of Jesus help enhance your understanding of God?

4. This chapter proposes that God as revealed in Jesus is forgiving, transforming, and ever-present. How might each of these attributes influence how you view God's activity in your life?

Chapter 4

Meeting Ourselves Again

When we moved into our present house, we brought several smaller pieces of outdoor equipment with us, among which was a moderately sized snow-blower. Fortunately for us, the previous owners of our house—ready to give up such extensive outdoor maintenance for the simpler life of condo living—also left us theirs, which included a more heavy duty snow-blower, a clear upgrade on the modest machine we brought with us. I was immediately grateful to receive this gift, as the smaller blower and I had not always been the best of friends over the years: it didn't seem to be able to handle more than a few inches, which has caused me to mutter some rather unspiritual things in its direction from time to time.

Despite living my entire life in the midwestern United States, I have not been a fan of snow for a very long while. The pitiful nature of my original snow-blower is but one small contributor to my dislike. I have been known in my household to go on extended rants about the quality and promptness of snow removal in my neighborhood and community on more than one occasion. The icy sheet that frequently hides underneath a new snow's powdery topmost layers has taken my feet out from under me more than once. I grumble at the wet, dirty, salt-encrusted mess that our shoes leave on our floors. I bristle at the unsafe conditions that a heavier snowfall creates for my family and for guests to our home. And while I appreciate the more powerful machine that allows me to clear my driveway, the wind often blows the snow right back at me, causing my face to feel like it's being hit by thousands of tiny frozen darts at once.

Every morning after a fresh snowfall, I wake up, look out the window, and silently shake my fist in irritation, knowing that once again I need to don several layers of clothing in order to deal with my flaky nemesis. Only the satisfaction of a job completed and a warm cup of coffee awaiting me afterward serves as motivation.

My son has a much different reaction to this intrusive precipitation. The sight of a new snowfall will send him running to the closet to grab his snow pants, coat, and boots while calling out repeated requests to see if the neighborhood kids want to play. Once he's outside, I watch as he and his friends pack it into fortresses or toss clumps at each other. He seems especially fascinated by how it tastes, and I have to remind him to go for the freshly-fallen clean stuff rather than that which has been turned other colors by varying causes. And, of course, there are the school cancellations, which for him bring the ultimate feeling of winter euphoria, while I scramble to rearrange my schedule to accommodate such a change.

Between the two of us, we have very different views of snow. To me, it is the source of inconvenience, annoyance, discomfort, and danger. To him, it provides a thousand opportunities for play that aren't possible during warmer seasons. How each of us perceives it affects how we approach it.

The Role of Our Own Experience

The previous chapter dealt with how our image of God influences how we approach our relationship with God. How we understand the divine transcendent to which we are connected is a key element in spirituality. In spiritual direction, this is a natural and expected conversation topic during each meeting. As has been discussed, answering, "Who is God for you?" is a recurring question in the spiritual direction relationship.

This question, however, is but one of several for our consideration. When we are engaged in spiritual reflection or practice, we are invited to pay greater attention to our own inner workings than on outer stimuli or concepts. In spiritual direction, the bigger concern is one's own reactions, emotions, affectations of personal identity, and so on. Our inner responses to our relationships with God, others, and ourselves, as well as how we perceive God's movement within them all, is that on which spiritual reflection and direction is based. Spirituality is as much about our image and awareness of ourselves as it is about our image of God, because we are the ones discerning both.

Karl Rahner notes that the nature of conceptualizing who God is carries with it the inevitable and concurrent task of conceptualizing who we are. As discussed in chapter 1, Rahner defines grace as God's self-communication; the gift of God's presence itself. By this definition, we are not meant to receive such a gift as an abstract image set apart from our own experience. Rather, this gift provides a starting point for how we might consider this divine self-communication making itself known in our lives and its particular circumstances.[1] In other words, our own experience of God—God's presence and activity in our specific history and present situation—is the true beginning point of what we are encouraged to consider in spiritual direction.

In order to put our experience in proper perspective, Rahner teaches, we must strive for a thorough understanding of our own identity. To a certain extent, this becomes a "chicken-and-egg" issue: our experience of God influences our sense of self, and our sense of self affects how we perceive God with us and in the world around us. But as the experiencer and perceiver, we ultimately must be conscious of our own lenses through which we make our interpretation.[2] Pursuit of such awareness involves careful consideration of how and why we may see or hear God working in any particular way. What is it about our own situation, family history, emotional state, faith background, and self-awareness, among so many other factors personal to each one of us, that may lead us to draw certain conclusions about God's presence with us?

Consider the difference in how I perceive snow as opposed to how my son sees it. I, as a homeowner who cares about his driveway being clear and his floors looking nice, is concerned about safety and accessibility issues related to walking and driving, and is admittedly self-conscious about what others may think or say about how well we keep up such things, sees snow as a nuisance to be removed as quickly as possible for both my own satisfaction and to ensure safe and easy passage for cars and walkers. My son, as a young child still discovering the world and attracted more to the many ways snow provides him enjoyment, sees it as something to mold, throw, lie in, and occasionally eat. The way we each perceive the same wintry occurrence affects how we experience it and how we understand our relationship to it, which ends up being very different according to our own concerns, needs, and desires. We interpret what snow is and what it means to each of us through our own lenses.

For this same reason cultivating a healthy awareness of ourselves becomes an important component in spirituality, and why spiritual direction will regularly invite such self-exploration. What brings us joy and anxiety—the source of which could be lingering memories or current situations involving relationships, work, finances, disease, and a host of other possible causes—affects us spiritually. These memories influence the questions we ask and the conclusions we draw. They affect how or whether we see God around us and within us. Our religious upbringing or lack thereof are not the only contributors to our spiritual perception. Rather, all of life together influences how we make meaning for ourselves, and thus paying attention to the many possible factors in our own lives helps us identify their spiritual dimension.

Naming the images of God with which we operate and in which we find meaning is important, but it is equally important to consider how we experience them in our lives and how and why they are meaningful. As the recipient of God's self-communication, how do we interpret that communication? We must also ask about the root causes of our interpretation; what past and current sources of pain and joy shape our response to the world, and our sense of God within it. What within us helps or hinders our "hearing" of what God is saying in any given moment? Seeking answers to these sorts of questions involves careful attention to how our past and present affects our interior life and our experience of God.

Breathing Freely

I've always had difficulty relying on others. I can be quite hesitant to ask for help or to express concerns that I have even to those I love and trust the most. This probably has multiple causes at its root, among them being the several moves that I experienced growing up. My father was a pastor, and starting over in new places is a regular feature of that familial lifestyle. I changed school systems when I was in 2nd grade, and again when I was in 7th. Both of these brought their own challenges in terms of re-orienting in a new situation, but as one might imagine, the junior high years are an especially difficult and brutal time of transition and socialization on their own, even without becoming acclimated to a new community of people on top of everything else.

These significant changes during my formative years contributed to a sense of self-reliance. Both consciously and subconsciously, I decided that I could and should handle problem-solving on my own, mainly with my own mental and emotional resources to guide me. Don't get me wrong: I did rely on parents, friends, and others for advice and assistance along the way, but for this reason and for others, I developed quite an independent streak. Heavy amounts of pride, internalization, and introversion mixed themselves into this cocktail of pigheadedness as well, all to fulfill my own felt need for self-preservation against the inevitability of change, as well as to avoid seeming helpless or weak to others. I can handle it, I tell myself, because I've handled it before.

This mindset has persisted in some form up to the present day. While again, I've never completely isolated myself from others, there nevertheless have been times when I continue to insist that I can deal with a problem without turning to others for expertise, resources, or support. This has played out as one might expect many times, with me only admitting that I need someone else after I've already tried and failed on my own.

Jaco Hamman observes that we each have a false self and a true self. The true self is our personal or private self, which is our expression of creativity and individuality. This self is the internal space where our authentic desires and ambitions reside. Largely due to environmental factors, however, we learn to suppress our true self and develop a false self as well. Our false self might also be called our "socialized self," the self that we project as our public persona, often against our genuine wishes or needs. It is the product of messages that we have internalized from our family, culture, and even the religious tradition with which we're most familiar. Our false self is who we believe the world wants us to be; what will help us receive praise and admiration.[3] Our false self is a contract we've been conditioned to think that we need to make with others: if I set aside who I really am and what I really want in order to seem secure to you, you will love me in return.

The primary concern of the false self is survival. We produce it because we believe it is what will earn us love from God, from others, and even from ourselves. It helps us feel safe in a world that we have experienced to be uncertain and cruel. It is the mask that we feel we need to wear to get through each day. At times, breathing in the mask is difficult: it becomes too stifling and limiting. We may become aware of how much our false self constricts our ability to live and breathe freely, but we may be so used to wearing it that we don't know how to remove it.

In my own case, my false self is one who can handle any difficulty on my own if I just think about it long enough or if I plug away at trial and error until a solution finally arises. My false self strives to avoid looking foolish, helpless, or unknowledgeable, lest I become an inconvenience to someone else or lose status in their eyes. The belief at the core of my false self is that both God and others will find me acceptable if I just work out my issues on my own. My mask restricts my ability to breathe in the sense that I don't ease my burden by sharing it with others.

In the spiritual life, we are always in pursuit of our true selves. We are invited to identify who we truly are and who we are meant to become. In spiritual direction, such identification involves exploring several aspects of ourselves at once. The first is to consider the implications of God's gift of gracious presence, already given to us before we had sought it or become conscious of it. No contract is issued to us in order to earn it; no mask given from God to wear in order to be considered acceptable and beloved. We have already been named as such, and the resultant transformation is a response rather than a pre-condition. Part of our true self is that we are already God's beloved children. We are invited to see ourselves as God sees us, and to live into what that means.

Often, the discovery or acceptance of our true self involves a long and often painful process of naming the origin and expression of the false self. This process can be difficult for several reasons, the first being that we may not even be aware of our own attitudes and practices that present it. So much of our false self is rooted in our subconscious, buried deep under messages that we've been hearing and living with for as long as we can remember. We could be acting out of a sense of social survival that we've carried with us since our earliest memories, and not be aware of the specifics of their development, how the cultivation of our false self is negatively impacting our own spirit or of those around us, or of the possibility that something could be different.

Fortunately, a host of resources are at our disposal to open us to an awareness of our false self. Assessment tools such as the Myers-Briggs, Enneagram, and Johari Window personality tests may help give insight to who we are, how we project ourselves, and how others perceive us.[4] Asking for honest appraisals from or simply sharing our story with trusted figures such as family members, friends, mentors, colleagues, counselors, pastors, or spiritual directors will provide feedback about how we present ourselves that we can't see on our own. Finally, a variety of spiritual practices and disciplines that open our heart-space enough to listen to God's presence with us may lead to revelations about how we are called to let go of who we've been to make room for something different. I call this process painful because realizations about how we treat others and how we treat ourselves under the oppressive weight of our false self can be difficult to receive, let alone act upon for release or change.

Several times in scripture, God's Spirit is closely associated with breath. When God creates the man in Genesis 2, God breathes the breath of life into him. In the prophet's vision of the valley of bones in Ezekiel 37, God breathes life back into the dusty human remains found there. In the Gospel of John's account of Jesus' first appearance to the disciples after the resurrection, he breathes on them and says, "Receive the Holy Spirit" (John 20:22). The Hebrew word *ruach* and the Greek *pneuma* can both mean either spirit or breath, and these accounts illustrate how closely linked they are.

The truth at the center of our true selves is that we are God-breathed. God has given us life, and wants us to fully live rather than merely survive. As we work to name our false self, admit to its destructive power, and begin the process of living into how God sees us, the first step has already been taken through God's grace-filled presence within us. Donning the mask of our false self restricts our breathing, and our ability to live as our true selves. God calls to us to remove our masks and to live as we were meant to live.

Whenever I have veered too far into yet another bout of trying to solve every problem on my own, among the reminders that I am given is the fact that others really do want to help. With this comes a realization that such help is being offered out of a genuine love and concern, a desire to receive an account of what I am facing so that others can show that love. My false self is neither needed nor appreciated by those who love me. God has no need for false selves, either. Rather, God sees us as we truly are: beloved, graced, God-breathed.

Done with False Narratives

Among his many parables, Jesus tells at least one that illustrates the importance of self-examination:

> *He also told this parable to some who trusted in themselves that they were righteous and regarded others with contempt: "Two men went up to the temple to pray, one a Pharisee and the other a tax collector. The Pharisee, standing by himself, was praying thus, 'God I thank you that I am not like other people: thieves, rogues, adulterers, or even like this tax collector. I fast twice a week; I give a tenth of all my income.' But the tax collector, standing far off, would not even look up to heaven, but was beating his breast and saying, 'God, be merciful to me, a sinner!' I tell you, this man went down to his home justified rather than the other; for all who exalt themselves will be humbled, but all who humble themselves will be exalted."* (Luke 18:9–14 NRSV)

In this brief story, two men go to the temple to pray. The writer of Luke frames the intent of this parable for us before he even begins: we are told at the outset in verse 9 that Jesus will use this short tale to make a point about some who see themselves who have an overdeveloped sense of self-worth while regarding others with disdain.

First, we meet the Pharisee. Pharisees were a religious group within first-century Judaism who were reformers in many ways. Rather than emphasizing the practice of temple worship, which simply would not have been possible after its destruction in the year 70 C.E., they believed that the observance of holiness should be integrated into all aspects of life.[5] Moreover, they were a group extremely dedicated to ritualistic purity, particularly in the midst of Roman occupation where living distinctly in a culture that did not share their beliefs and practices became all the more important.

The Pharisee, we are told, stands apart by himself. He prays thus: "God, I thank you that I am not like other people: thieves, rogues, adulterers, or even like this tax collector. I fast twice a week; I give a tenth of all my income" (Luke 18:11b-12). He begins by thanking God, but for what? That he has been able to avoid the same temptations, shortcomings, desperation, and compromise that has befallen so many of those around him. He lists a few of his practices of faithfulness to drive home how devout he is: he does the right things and avoids the wrong things. "God," he says, "it's good to be me."

While the Pharisee at least begins to give God the credit, and in his day he would have been honored for his faithfulness, his prayer nevertheless reveals a glimpse of who his false self might be: one who believes he is above those less fortunate or whose flaws are more easily detected. While he begins by thanking God, the rest of his prayer is a list of his own accomplishments. His inclusion of some of the ways he faithfully observes religious obligation by tithing and fasting hints at a felt need to earn God's favor. He exalts himself, which is the attitude against which Jesus warns at the end of his parable. His false self mask might be naming his own goodness in comparison to others so as to earn approval.

The tax collector's posture is very different. He is contrite and perhaps frightened, not even able to bring himself to lift his head. His prayer is shorter and more straightforward: "God, be merciful to me, a sinner" (Luke 18:13). Those who originally heard this parable would have had a certain idea about the tax collector: they were agents of the oppressive Roman state, seen as betrayers to their own people by virtue of their role in the Empire. They were also scam artists, collecting far more than was required in order to line their own pockets, exploiting those who didn't have much to give to begin with. Jesus' original audience would not have had many good things to say about the tax collector.

As it turns out, neither does the tax collector himself. He can only manage to utter a single line. Whereas the Pharisee spends all of his time listing his good deeds, the tax collector can only ask for mercy. He seems to be very aware of how he has used his position to his own advantage, and it's all he can do to cower in the hope that God has even a morsel of forgiveness to spare.

Jesus favors the behavior of the tax collector in his parable, casting him as the one humbling himself over and against the self-exalting Pharisee. The tax collector "gets it," while his counterpart does not. His prayer seems to be a moment of rock bottom, where he is ready to take on a different way of interacting with himself and the world. Perhaps this is his turning point, where he gives up his former ways, begins reconciling with those from whom he has stolen, and embarks on a new life. His false self, perhaps hiding behind the authority of his position, may now begin to give way to living more honestly, forsaking the economic violence from which he had been benefitting. All this time his mask might be one of hiding behind his position to look out for his own interests. The origin of his true self is in his acknowledgment of God as a giver of mercy. His journey of seeing himself and others as God sees him is just beginning.

Each of the characters in this story are dealing with their own false narrative. The Pharisee's is a narrative of self-aggrandizement, where his own pure behavior carries the day and he needs God's rubber stamp of approval on who he is. The tax collector's is one of self-preservation, where he bends and exploits the rules to fulfill his own wants at others' expense. They have each been conditioned by the same social and cultural conditions to behave as they do and construct their false selves accordingly. There is hope for each to embrace their true selves, as there is for all of us.

A colleague and I met for our latest in a series of spiritual direction meetings. I was guiding her through Ignatius of Loyola's

Spiritual Exercises, which early in the process invites the person making the journey to reflect on sin: its overall concept, its effect on the individual going through the Exercises, and God's love for the person regardless.

The person with whom I was meeting was experiencing nearly every major life transition one could imagine at once: she was going through divorce proceedings with her husband, her mother after a long illness had passed away, and she was facing questions about her future career path. Along with these transitions came many questions about her own self-worth, and where and how God was showing divine love and making room for peace in the midst of it. Finally, a few weeks into the Exercises' focus on sin, she announced, "I'm done with guilt and shame. I've been feeling enough of it from other places and from other people, and it's not what I need from this."

My directee was fed up with living in a false narrative. Her false self mask up to that point might have been to believe and accept the shame of others. But she recognized that, while these life changes were heavy loads to bear and brought mixed reactions from those around her, she was not to remain in a place of disgrace, nor a view of herself forever marked by stigma and stress. There would be a new narrative to replace the old, one in which she was already God's beloved child, where her true self, born of grace, could begin to thrive.

In her spiritual classic *Interior Castle,* Teresa of Avila invites the reader to think of the spiritual life as journeying through a series of seven rooms within a castle, with each closer to the center of one's soul than the last. This soul-castle is not mere stone and mortar, but rather like a radiant crystal, complex and awe-inspiring and inviting exploration. This castle is a wonderful paradise, made in God's image and carved with great care and delight.[6] Unfortunately, she observes, not many seem very interested in exploring the rooms of the soul. Many seem much more content to remain in the courtyard, giving little thought to what might be inside. She laments, "there are souls so infirm and so accustomed to busying themselves with outside affairs that nothing can be done for them, and it seems as though they are incapable of entering within themselves at all."[7] Many have been dealing in false narratives and projecting a false self for so long that the prospect of self-examination is too daunting and could bring too much pain. What might we discover if we venture inside? What true self awaits us, longing for freedom?

While such a process of identity and discovery carries immense uncertainty, it begins with God's gift of self-communicated presence and grace. God already sees us as beloved children, even if we insist on trying to forge our own contracts with God instead. Breaking down the barriers of our false selves and beginning the journey toward what is true takes a great amount of courage, prayer, and reflection. Spiritual direction invites us beyond the courtyard to see ourselves as God sees us.

Questions for reflection

1. How do you think your image or images of God affect how you see yourself? How does your sense of self influence your image of God? What elements from your experience, whether from your past or in more recent times, have contributed to each?

2. Take time to reflect on how you present yourself to others. What social factors, perhaps from your upbringing, have contributed to this presentation. How would you characterize your false self? What do you feel the need to wall off from others? What is your false self's contract with God ("I will be your child if . . .")?

3. Try sitting down with someone you trust, asking them to give an honest assessment of how they see you. How much is what they offer the same or different from how you see yourself? What do you find affirming, surprising, or challenging about what they say?

4. Consider the difference between how God sees you and how you see yourself. How far apart would you say these images are? Consider again the prayers offered by the Pharisee and tax collector, and the self-images that inspired them. Compose your own prayer that you think helps name your desire to find your true self in light of God's grace.

Chapter 5

Beginning to Listen

The past two chapters have invited us to consider our images of both God and ourselves. In the cultivation of our spiritual life, we first consider the images and metaphors we find most meaningful as we relate to God. Whether positive or negative, these images affect how we see our own identity in relationship to God and God's world. Any intentional attempt at spiritual formation will include reflection on our experience of God in our own lives in their particularity. Interweaving the two themes of God and self is the premise on which spiritual direction is based. Thus a spiritual director observes back to us what he or she sees as our operating images transform, evolve, expand, and deepen depending on circumstances, life events, and revelations along the way.

Having engaged in reflection on the images with which we tend to work as a starting point, we turn now to some of the ways by which our images may undergo such transformation. Since the earliest days of human spiritual understanding, a wide variety of practices and rituals have helped mediate and communicate a tradition's individual and communal images of God and self. From the primitive religion of humanity's earliest days, to Eastern forms at the root of modern Hinduism, to the Hebrew Tabernacle and Israelite Temple, to the polytheistic Western temples of Ancient Greece, and on down through the ages, we have always sought ways to clarify and nurture our understanding of the transcendent's presence among us.

As in these other religions, Christianity has benefited from a richness of prayer traditions unique to its beliefs over the centuries. These prayers have grown out of the deep faith of many devoted followers such as the Desert Fathers and Mothers, Ignatius of Loyola, Francis and Clare of Assisi, and Benedict of Nursia, as well as Protestant spiritual expressions that we know today as Lutheran, Reformed, Wesleyan, and Pentecostalism, among so many others.

Given the multiple and diverse opportunities for spiritual formation that Christian believers have inherited throughout our history, we are invited to consider our beliefs surrounding prayer: what we believe it does, and how we practice it as a result. A spiritual director may regularly ask those with whom he or she meets, "How's your prayer life?" What we believe about the purpose of prayer, as well as our chosen method and frequency, serve to nurture our sense of God's presence. Prayer practices are the tools that we use to build on this awareness, so it is important to explore what we believe about its function, as well as open ourselves to new ways of practicing it.

Quick to Listen, Slow to Speak

A form of prayer familiar to many Christians is that of petition, a common element of many Sunday morning worship gatherings. In petition, we bring to God our concerns, worries, desires, and needs, and ask for some provision or response to them. We ask for a fresh sense of God's presence. We lift up loved ones who are sick or hurting. We pray for our own difficulties and doubts. We speak in the hope that God will listen and respond. We conclude these prayers with the words "your will be done" as a statement of faith that whatever happens will reflect God's purposes.

Prayers of petition are about we the petitioner saying what we've come to say before God. They can be helpful for our own spirits in that we speak aloud those concerns that are weighing most heavily upon us, as we trust that they are heard yet already known. Individuals and communities of faith name these concerns for themselves and each other, if for no other reason than to acknowledge that we are not alone in our struggle. When we speak the names of others for whom we worry, we do so wishing for a greater amount of divine attention and energy to be with them. For all these reasons and more, petition can be a powerful and meaningful form of prayer to practice on a regular basis.

However, there are several limitations to only practicing this form of prayer. The first is intention without follow-through. How often might a person of faith say to another, "I'll pray for you," and then neglect to do so? In many instances, this statement has become a pious version of "That's too bad," or "I hope things improve." Truly, this could be said about any form of prayer: the intention to practice it and then the failure to commit leads to little change for anyone.

A second limitation to only practicing petition is the lack of transformative potential that it holds for the one who does it. If we only take time to list for God our anxieties and desires, there is little chance that we may be inspired to change or respond. Telling God about our problems may help ease our sense of despair, but we may not take the time to consider how God may be calling us to be part of the solution. If, for instance, we pray for a friend who seems lonely or afraid, God might want us to offer our own presence in some way to help change his or her situation. If we only pray for them thinking that in doing so we've played our part, we risk missing out on how God is answering.

Finally, if we only speak during prayer, our conversation with God becomes incredibly one-sided. Prayer is as much about listening as it is about speaking. Making space within ourselves to listen for God's response carries with it the potential to have a much deeper and enriching prayer experience. Taking this time to listen; to consider how God is answering through a change of heart, call to action, or newfound sense of assurance or peace, is how prayer moves from only giving to also receiving.

Many traditions call listening prayer by different names, but I will focus on two: meditation and contemplation. These forms of prayer invite us to be silent and consider what God has to say to us, usually with the help of other material as a way of centering our attention and energy. It is first important to differentiate between what I mean by each.

Meditation, as defined by Michael Ivens, is more of a "thought prayer." That is, it uses material as guidance in order to imagine or think through something in light of one's faith and strive to listen to how God is speaking (specifically to the one praying). In some forms of this type of prayer, the material on which one is meditating might be related to a general truth such as grace, sin, material attachment, justice, or love.[1] At other times, one may be invited to focus on a general image like the beat of his or her heart, imagine a ball of energy relaxing each muscle group in turn, or envision one's connection to the universe in different ways.

Ignatius of Loyola features a series of meditations in his Spiritual Exercises, inviting the one meditating to imagine various scenarios and to think about how they help the person make sense of general truths or images such as those mentioned above. For instance, his meditation called The Triple Colloquy invites the one praying to imagine a conversation with Jesus during which he or she shares their shortcomings and struggles with temptations, and expresses an increased desire to resist the pull of the world toward selfishness, greed, and vanity. This meditation emphasizes that such a conversation happen in a natural way as if talking to a friend. Many Ignatian meditations follow a similar pattern of mentally entering into a scene so as to notice one's own reactions to them. The purpose of this type of prayer is greater insight into what a relationship with God entails.

Meditation is a good entry point into prayerful listening. It helps one who is new to the practice create a sanctuary within the heart; thus making the emotional and spiritual space needed for further listening to God's call.[2] Thomas Merton notes that meditation is less about devising a method or system and more about cultivating an attitude. What we learn and discern through meditation over time becomes a part of us, and we increasingly live according to God's guiding presence in the world.³ The materials on which we meditate serve the greater purpose of making room inside ourselves to hear God speaking to us, whether we are actively and consciously praying or not.

This leads us to a second form of prayer known as contemplation. In contrast with meditation, which begins more with intellectual faculties, contemplation makes greater use of our emotions. In contemplation we consider how we are affected by elements within and around us as they reflect God's presence. Whereas with meditation we are meant to focus our energies on a large truth within the Christian tradition and how it applies to us, the object of contemplation is simpler, yet more complex: our inner emotions and God's presence with us.⁴

Ignatius also encouraged the use of contemplation using stories from the Christian scriptures as a medium through which God speaks. Just as he encouraged the thoughtful entry into scenarios proposed in his meditations, he also encourages imaginative entry into Biblical stories, particularly those about Jesus. The idea behind this practice is to find ways to make these memories become alive for us as believers today. God reaches out to us through these narratives, speaking fresh words to those who spend time with them.⁵ In contemplation, we seek to experience the stories: what they look, sound, smell, and feel like, rather than to inquire about their historical background, doctrinal significance, or moral implications. To contemplate them is to allow God to happen to us through them.

And yet, this exercise is but one form of contemplation. As with meditation, it is a means to a deeper form of prayerful attentiveness to and love for God. It is not just through scripture that God speaks, although that is a primary medium through which we may discern the divine voice. God may also speak through music, a loved one's embrace, the sight of a clear night sky, the bustling of a coffeehouse, the aroma of freshly baked bread, the savoring of wine shared with friends. Contemplation presupposes that God's activity underlies all of these experiences. As Merton suggests, contemplation is a kind of "spiritual vision" to which we aspire using all our intellectual and emotional faculties. Contemplation is the development of a different way of seeing the world in all its God-saturated nature.[6] It is less something we achieve by our own effort, and more an awareness that grows within us over time.

Both meditation and contemplation employ the gifts of reason and emotion that God has already given to us in order to listen for the many other gifts that God means to give. They open us to listen for how God speaks through all of life, beginning with the materials of our own Christian tradition, but also radiating outward into every moment of our existence.

Before going much further, several caveats regarding these forms of prayer warrant mentioning. First, while in general terms meditation has been cast here as more cerebral and contemplation more affective, both contain elements of the other. Emotions help us to personalize our reflections, and reason helps us make sense of what we feel and why. So I don't mean to imply a clean and absolute separation between the two.

Second, I wish to reiterate that these forms of prayer require regular practice for them to take root within us. They will not necessarily produce spectacular or obvious revelations every time we observe them, especially if we only do so between extended intervals. Listening prayer makes room within us to hear or experience God, but we may not have an experience that is overt or obvious every time. As with any spiritual practice, intentionality and patience are integral to these prayer forms as we cultivate a new way of seeing God at work in the world and within ourselves.

Using Our Imagination

In discussing these methods of prayer, I have mentioned the imagination several times. This demands further explanation, as the concept of using the imagination in prayer may seem out of place; foreign to such an exercise. We may not tend to associate the imagination with our pursuit of the sacred because it may seem too subjective; given to our own biases and whims. After all, if we are invited to imagine as part of our prayer, what would prevent us from concocting the conclusion we desire, bending the exercise to suit our own ends?

True enough, there is danger in suggesting that we make the imagination an active part of discerning God's presence with us. So let me clarify what I mean when I encourage its use. First, some might suggest that the imagination is unreliable due to its subjective nature; the intellect is much more capable of judging between truth and our own wishes. However, we are just as capable of rationalizing what we want to be true; bending logic to suit our own needs. What purports to be a purely cerebral approach still needs a counterpoint in order to evaluate its reliability. The support of others such as a spiritual director or a discerning faith community helps meet this need..

Second, both the imagination and intellect are valid parts of our human experience. The former is a gift of creativity, stemming from the One who created all that we know and haven't yet discovered. The latter is a gift of evaluation and meaning-making, also from the same divine Source. Both gifts combine to assist us in making sense of who God is for us and who we are in relation to that divine identity. As has been discussed in the previous two chapters, we use images as part of this process of exploration, whether we are conscious of this or not.

Finally, when we are invited to imagine in prayer, another word might be "envision." As part of his instructions in the Spiritual Exercises, Ignatius of Loyola often encourages people to "picture the place" when preparing to contemplate a story from scripture. He urges them to envision the scene as completely as possible, down to details such as facial expressions, the dust on the ground, the feel of the walls in a house. Using the imagination in this way helps us enter more completely into the narrative and experience it for ourselves. This is why these forms of prayer often use a specific scene to help focus our reflection. We use our imagination in order to envision ourselves in God's story, rather than make up God's place in ours.

Jesus himself understood this, as storytelling was a signature part of his earthly ministry. Often, in response to a question or when he otherwise wanted to make a point about God or discipleship or a new possible reality, he wouldn't deliver a straightforward theological treatise. Instead, he told parables: brief tales drawing from elements of life that people knew well. These were a source of frustration to both disciples and critics alike, who repeatedly would request that he explain what he meant. At times, as with the so-called parable of the sower found in Matthew, Mark, and Luke, he obliges (or at least the Gospel writers take their best shot). Much more often, however, he simply tells a story and then moves onto another town, another teaching, another healing, another meal.

When heard through ears of the culture in which they were originally told, Jesus' parables become even more intriguing and provocative. The Biblical scholar C.H. Dodd observed that these stories usually have a strangeness to them, which would have caused the original audience to doubt its clear application, and thus be left to ponder its meaning long after its narrator had finished.[7]

One of Jesus' best-known parables, for instance, is the story of the "good Samaritan" from the Gospel of Luke:

> *Just then a lawyer stood up to test Jesus. "Teacher," he said, "what must I do to inherit eternal life?" He said to him, "What is written in the law? What do you read there?" He answered, "You shall love the Lord your God with all your heart, and with all your soul, and with all your strength, and with all your mind; and your neighbor as yourself." And he said to him, "You have given the right answer; do this and you will live."*

> *But wanting to justify himself, he asked Jesus, "And who is my neighbor?" Jesus replied, "A man was going down from Jerusalem to Jericho, and fell into the hands of robbers, who stripped him, beat him, and went away, leaving him half dead. Now by chance a priest was going down that road; and when he saw him, he passed by on the other side. So likewise a Levite, when he came to the place and saw him, passed by on the other side. But a Samaritan while traveling came near him; and when he saw him, he was moved with pity. He went to him and bandaged his wounds, having poured oil and wine on them. Then he put him on his own animal, brought him to an inn, and took care of him. The next day he took out two denarii, gave them to the innkeeper, and said, 'Take care of him; and when I come back, I will repay you whatever more you spend.' Which of these three, do you think, was a neighbor to the man who fell into the hands of the robbers?" He said, "The one who showed him mercy." Jesus said to him, "Go and do likewise."* (Luke 10:25–37 NRSV)

Here a lawyer approaches Jesus to ask how far-reaching the commandment to love your neighbor as yourself actually is. Jesus tells this story in response to the question, "Who is my neighbor?"

Jesus sets up the scene with a man robbed on a dangerous road and left for dead in a ditch. Two dedicated religious figures whom perhaps the audience figured beforehand would have foregone any kind of assistance moved as far away from the helpless soul and continued on their way. So next, a Samaritan rounds the bend, sees the man in need, tends to his wounds, and puts him up for a while at an inn.

We modern hearers have been conditioned to read this parable as a moral example story and little more: "help other people like the Samaritan did." But as soon as the Samaritan showed up, the original hearers would have stopped cold. Due to sharp religious and cultural differences, Jews and Samaritans didn't get along. These groups steered clear of each other as much as possible. And yet, to an audience likely made up largely of Jews, Jesus makes a Samaritan the hero of his story in answering someone who wants to know, "Who is my neighbor?"

Because he adds this strange detail to his story, Jesus leaves his hearers to wrestle with its meaning. Its unconventional quality causes it to linger in their thoughts, drawing them deeper into the story to consider how they are a part of it. Are they really meant to act like the Samaritan? Could their possible reaction to this character's inclusion make them more like the Priest or Levite who want nothing to do with the person whimpering for help? Could they one day be the helpless one who might need someone whom they'd otherwise avoid to stop and provide assistance? Who are we in God's story; who are we meant to be? As we prayerfully listen for God to speak through the strange and surprising details of scripture, the answer might not be what we expected.

Think of a time when you read a novel and could identify with a particular character in some way. Maybe it was the situation in which they found themselves, details of their background, or certain traits they exhibit as they move through the story. Perhaps you've experienced this with a character in a movie or TV show rather than a book. Or think of a time when a certain song seemed to speak to your unique circumstances, naming your feelings of joy, sadness, helplessness, or excitement as if it had been written just for you in that moment. On the other hand, maybe it wasn't that we could already see ourselves in these stories, but were able to feel what the actor or singer was feeling; journeying beyond the limitations of what we know in order to understand the thoughts and emotions within the story being told.

When this happens, it is because we are able to envision ourselves in the story. We forge a connection with its subject because we can imagine how they are describing life either as we have known it, or some new truth about life that we have not yet known. In this way, we already use the sort of envisioning that may deepen and enrich our awareness of ourselves within God's story as explored in listening prayer.

Seeing the Place, Seeing Ourselves

At the beginning of many of his guidelines for praying with a scriptural story, Ignatius of Loyola offers what he calls three preludes for the purposes of focusing on the task at hand. The first prelude he calls the history, which is the specific scene from the Gospels being considered. The second he calls the composition, or seeing the place. Here we are invited to imagine the scene as vividly as we can: the width of a road, the pottery on a shelf, the emotions felt by the people involved, the smells of the marketplace. Whatever is pertinent to the scene, we are encouraged to envision it in detail so as to truly experience it, as well as notice our reactions to it. Finally, the third prelude is to ask for what we want, which is usually greater clarity about a particular gift from God within us. Depending on how far we are through the Exercises, we might ask for awareness of God's love for us despite our own sin or shortcomings, a desire to follow Jesus as a disciple or servant, sorrow at his crucifixion, or joy at the resurrection.

The key to this form of prayer is the composition. During the history, we may recall facts about the focus scripture or study it as if in an educational setting. But it is in the composition, the seeing the place, where the Spirit creates meaning for us in the present moment, whether about God, ourselves, or both. Seeing the place and noticing our own thoughts and emotions in the midst of the story helps make it personal to us.[8]

I was offering spiritual direction to a woman who was journeying through an 8-week version of Ignatius' Spiritual Exercises. We had met a few times by that point, and she was just beginning several weeks that focused on stories of Jesus' ministry: his interactions, healings, teachings, and parables. We had talked about the use of imagination as a way of entering into the story and prayerfully listening for God through the words, paying special attention to her own reactions, emotions, and senses as she read.

One story suggested for a particular week was that of Jesus visiting Mary and Martha from Luke 10:38–42, where Mary sits at Jesus' feet while Martha is busy with many obligations and chores around the house. Exasperated that she is left to do everything herself, Martha finally implores Jesus to have Mary get up and help her, only to have Jesus chide her for her busyness and distraction while commending Mary for her choice to sit and listen to him. Guidelines for imaginative prayer in hand, my directee set off for the week to try things out.

During our next meeting, she seemed especially affected by her experience with this story. She had felt led to observe this scene as a bystander rather as one of the characters, and had a strong reaction to Jesus' response to Martha: "I actually found myself saying to him, 'Now, hold on a minute. There's a lot to do! Martha needs help!'" We explored the nature of this reaction; what inside my directee might have caused her to say what she said. Among other things, she has a very strong work ethic that would have led her to join in with Martha's to-do list. We also talked about the importance of taking time to sit, rest, and reflect in Jesus' presence. She heard something of herself by envisioning the story, and spiritual direction helped her explore its possible meaning and what God might be saying to her, both in affirming her need to complete tasks and also in the possibilities that pausing more often to notice the presence of God's gift of grace in her life could bring for her spiritual growth.

Ignatius appreciated the imagination as a gift from God to be treasured and used, rather than minimized or avoided. He discovered its potential for helping us envision the stories of scripture and thereby achieve a heightened awareness of God's presence. This sort of prayerful exercise gives us a greater capacity for listening for God's message to us.

One may hesitate to attempt this sort of prayer practice for multiple reasons. Perhaps you have only known a particular form of prayer based on speaking your concerns to God. Perhaps the use of the imagination in this way seems strange or awkward. Perhaps your concerns are more practical, such as uncertainty about a regular time and place to observe it. You may not be sure how to process what happens during your prayer, or whether anything will happen at all. It may be that some aspect of your image of God or your self-image may be preventing you from starting. Perhaps you see God as distant or harsh, or you've internalized an identity that causes you to wonder whether you'd truly be heard.

As we have seen, naming the images discussed in the previous chapter is important, because they shape how one conceptualizes the divine-human relationship and, in turn, how one engages in it. Certain images of God and self may cause us to pray fearfully, or only in the language of poetic piety, or with a resigned skepticism. The forms of prayer discussed in this chapter are grounded in certain images. They assume that God chooses to be in close, purposeful relationship with us out of love and self-giving grace, and sees us as worth engaging despite our imperfections. Prayer is yet another response to what God is already sharing with us.

A trusted guide such as a spiritual director may help us explore these issues. He or she is meant to serve as a non-judgmental and encouraging companion on the spiritual journey, helping to ease the feelings of anxiety, awkwardness, or self-doubt that are inevitable as one begins exploring meditation. He or she first serves to help the directee stay on task in observing a regular practice. Mostly, however, a spiritual director is called to listen to your experience and help identify where and how God may have been speaking through your thoughts and emotions while at prayer. More so, he or she may offer reminders that God wishes to speak and listen in this relationship as much as we do.

William Barry observes that even the simple act of talking about our prayer life with another helps us pay better attention to our relationship with God. Speaking our experience out loud allows another to hear, observe, repeat back, and ask questions.[9] In order to grow more deeply in your relationship with God, you might consider asking yourself the question mentioned at the beginning of this chapter, "How's your prayer life?" in order to listen more eagerly and attentively.

Questions for Reflection

1. How would you respond if you were asked, "How's your prayer life?" How would you describe your current practice of prayer? What do you find helpful? What would you want to improve?

2. How familiar are you with prayer forms such as meditation and contemplation? How have you seen them characterized by Christian and non-Christian spiritual traditions?

3. Think about the ways you currently use your imagination in your everyday life. Perhaps it's to solve a problem at your job, make plans for time away either by yourself or with loved ones, or while working on a personal creative project. We each have our own imaginative gifts depending on our interests. How could you see bringing your particular gifts to the practice of prayer?

4. Choose a story from the Gospels and try to envision it based on what is described in this chapter. What difference does it make in how you read the passage? What do you end up noticing that you might not have before? Who could you talk to about your experience?

Chapter 6

Propane Altars and Dishwasher Shrines

The previous chapter introduced two forms of prayer, meditation and contemplation, for which the emphases are upon listening and experience rather than speaking. As such, meditation regularly uses an imaginative exercise on which to focus in order to reflect on some aspect of God's nature or the way God wishes for us to live in the world. Meditation serves as a helpful introduction to this general method of prayer by increasing our familiarity and comfort levels with its practice. It encourages us to use mental pictures, noting the details of the scene and our own emotional reaction to them as a way of discerning God's presence and voice.

As Ignatius of Loyola encourages it, contemplation makes use of materials such as scripture passages as a beginning point for seeing God in the world around us. Rather than actively reflect on abstract concepts as in meditation, contemplation is the development of our ability to see God in all things. Practicing contemplation each day makes room within us for a new way of interacting with God's presence in all of creation.

Thomas Merton describes contemplation as a gift. An increased awareness of God around us is not achieved solely on our own efforts, but by the divine presence to which we become more open via regular prayerful observance. Neither is it achieved by intellectual pursuit alone; by holding within us certain ideas about God that we deem correct. Rather, contemplation entails a growing consciousness of God in relationship to our whole selves, to which we respond and upon which we act in the everyday occurrences that make up our days.[1]

One assumption behind the practice of contemplation is that God is always engaged in relationship with us, active alongside us in big and small ways, in moments we consider important and mundane. As we practice this form of prayer, over time we see the line between sacred and secular disappear as we become more cognizant of all parts of our lives graced by the gift of God's presence. Contemplation is a means to recognizing and celebrating this truth; living into it as fully as we are able at all times.

We have previously considered an image of God based upon the life and person of Jesus, highlighting three aspects of God's character which he embodies: forgiveness, transformation, and imminence. These are interrelated: through our active realization and acceptance of God's forgiveness, we are gratefully inspired to transform our outlook and behavior. As we are transformed, our awareness of God with us becomes ever more acute. God's presence itself is a gracious gift shared with us, which includes the enacting of forgiveness for what we consider unforgivable and the invitation to remove the mask of our false self.

God's imminence (immediate presence) serves as a beginning for these other characteristics, preceding any conscious reaction or acknowledgment on our part. As Karl Rahner observes, God initiates the divine-human relationship through God's absolute closeness and communication of God's self to us.[2] As 1 John declares, "we love because he first loved us" (1 John 4:19). God first shares in life with us, and invites our reciprocation.

Through contemplation and other means, we are ever discovering what God sharing life with us in this way means. For a variety of reasons, we may hesitate to discern God's imminent activity in all that we do. Why, we might ask, would God care enough to be a part of my Monday morning staff meeting, my raking the leaves, my dropping off my child at daycare, or my loading the dishwasher? Does God really think that showing up for these events or tasks is worthwhile? What would be the point?

And yet, if Jesus reveals to us a God who is ever-present, that presence extends to the most ordinary and frivolous actions of our day. After all, we read of him performing signs at weddings, in fishing boats, on hillsides, during meals, and in houses. His grand gestures of love and providence didn't happen nearly as often in venues especially set aside for the sacred, but in places where many found themselves most hours of the day. Jesus shows us a God who goes where we already are. If we want to believe that God cares about those times in our lives when we most need God to assure us that we are not alone, then why not also trust that God is sharing God's self with us in times less urgent and more commonplace? God is still loving, sharing, and self-communicating to us even then, because God means for this relationship to be constant and ongoing, rather than only brought out for special occasions like our grandmother's silverware. God wants our attention and is giving us attention in those other times as well.

To reflect further on God's constant self-communication, we turn to Psalm 139:

> *O LORD, you have searched me and known me.*
> *You know when I sit down and when I rise up;*
> *you discern my thoughts from far away.*
> *You search out my path and my lying down,*
> *and are acquainted with all my ways.*
> *Even before a word is on my tongue,*
> *O LORD, you know it completely.*
> *You hem me in, behind and before,*
> *and lay your hand upon me.*
> *Such knowledge is too wonderful for me;*
> *it is so high that I cannot attain it.*
> *Where can I go from your spirit?*
> *Or where can I flee from your presence?*
> *If I ascend to heaven, you are there;*
> *if I make my bed in Sheol, you are there.*
> *If I take the wings of the morning*

and settle at the farthest limits of the sea,
even there your hand shall lead me,
and your right hand shall hold me fast.
If I say, "Surely the darkness shall cover me,
and the light around me become night,"
even the darkness is not dark to you;
the night is as bright as the day,
for darkness is as light to you.
For it was you who formed my inward parts;
you knit me together in my mother's womb.
I praise you, for I am fearfully and wonderfully made.
Wonderful are your works;
that I know very well.
My frame was not hidden from you,
when I was being made in secret,
intricately woven in the depths of the earth.
Your eyes beheld my unformed substance.
In your book were written
all the days that were formed for me,
when none of them as yet existed.
How weighty to me are your thoughts, O God!
How vast is the sum of them!
I try to count them—they are more than the sand;
I come to the end—I am still with you.
O that you would kill the wicked, O God,
and that the bloodthirsty would depart from me—
those who speak of you maliciously,
and lift themselves up against you for evil!
Do I not hate those who hate you, O Lord*?*
And do I not loathe those who rise up against you?
I hate them with perfect hatred;
I count them my enemies.
Search me, O God, and know my heart;

> *test me and know my thoughts.*
> *See if there is any wicked way in me,*
> *and lead me in the way everlasting.* (Psalm 139 NRSV)

In verse 3 above, the psalmist writes, "You search out my path and my lying down, and are acquainted with all my ways." The verb "search" describes God as not merely present, but actively engaged in the psalmist's life. God seeks the psalmist wherever his path takes him, and when he stops to rest. Through this intentional pursuit, he writes, God is intimately connected to all that he does.

A few verses later, the psalmist poses a rhetorical question: "Where can I go from your spirit? Or where can I flee from your presence" (Psalm 139:7)? No matter where the writer ends up—heaven or the place of the dead, the farthest reaches of the horizon—God will always hold him close. There is no place where the psalmist can go that is foreign or off-limits to God. There is no place unimportant enough, no action small enough, that causes God to wait further off for the psalmist to get back to more pressing matters. God also chooses to go to those places simply because that's where the subject of God's communication is going. God wants to be where the writer is, no matter what.

And why might this be? The writer explores that, too: "For it was you who formed my inward parts; you knit me together in my mother's womb. I praise you, for I am fearfully and wonderfully made. Wonderful are your works; that I know very well" (Psalm 139:13–14). God is the creator of all humanity, each individual knitted together with care, awe, and wonder. God has known the psalmist since his earliest beginning, and continues to know all he is and does.

God knows us and searches us out wherever we go. To some this may sound threatening and intrusive: do we really want God around all the time? If we operate with an image of God who watches for our every misstep, keeping a tally of every sin and shortcoming, God's involvement with our lives every second of the day may not seem very affirming. But judgment is not God's primary intention. As Jesus shows us, God's presence is a gracious gift. God does intend our transformation; our turning from the damage we do to ourselves and others. God does not do this out of malicious or punitive intent. Rather, God knows us and wants us to be who we really are; to drop the stifling masks of our false self and live as beloved and God-breathed creatures, fearfully and wonderfully made.

Lifting the Veil

We've discussed at some length now how the practice of listening forms of prayer may help us discern God's self-communication to us in the world. Still, we may have difficulty seeing how God is in all things around us. While prayer involves time, effort, focus, and intentionality, we may wonder how that translates to cleaning our bathroom, buying groceries, driving to work, or weeding our garden. After all, our schedules can be full, and these tasks aren't going to do themselves. How, then, might we cultivate an awareness of God's presence during these times?

In 2 Corinthians, Paul reflects on the veils we wear:

> *Since, then, we have such a hope, we act with great boldness, not like Moses, who put a veil over his face to keep the people of Israel from gazing at the end of the glory that was being set aside. But their minds were hardened. Indeed, to this very day, when they hear the reading of the old covenant, that same veil is still there, since only in Christ is it set aside. Indeed, to this very day whenever Moses is read, a veil lies over their minds; but when one turns to the Lord, the veil is removed. Now the Lord is the Spirit, and where the Spirit of the Lord is, there is freedom. And all of us, with unveiled faces, seeing the glory of the Lord as though reflected in a mirror, are being transformed*

into the same image from one degree of glory to another; for this comes from the Lord, the Spirit.

Therefore, since it is by God's mercy that we are engaged in this ministry, we do not lose heart. We have renounced the shameful things that one hides; we refuse to practice cunning or to falsify God's word; but by the open statement of the truth we commend ourselves to the conscience of everyone in the sight of God. (2 Corinthians 3:12–4:2)

The veil that Paul talks about here is different from the mask of the false self, as the latter is something that we wear for the world around us; a result of wanting to be who we think others want us to be. Instead, Paul uses a veil metaphor to talk about how we see God in the world, rather than how we want the world to see us.

Paul first reinterprets a story from Exodus 34, in which Moses has spent so long on Mount Sinai talking to God that when he returns to the people, he has to wear a veil to shield them from the brilliant shine that he's acquired on his face. Paul suggests that we are all wearing veils over our minds, unable to see God's presence and glory revealed to us in Christ through God's Spirit. Christ is the one to whom we turn to see God.

Paul's discussion of veils may invite a few questions. Does lifting the veil happen all at once, where we suddenly and fully see God at work in every time and situation and moment? Or is the lifting of the veil happen more gradually, where we catch glimpses when we're intentionally looking for them; keyed in on God's Spirit with us?

Life experience seems to favor the latter. Let's be honest: God seems elusive at times. Some might say that God seems elusive the majority of the time, especially in those inevitable moments of hardship, grief, despair, and loss. It may be easy for the psalmist to extol the many places God follows us and the many ways God knows us, but harder for us to consider how that is so. Whatever prayer practice we observe, we might spend part of that time asking how God is with us. These questions are honest and worthwhile, and we should not refrain from asking them. In fact, the writers of the Psalms asked them on a regular basis. If God searches us out and knows us, then that includes our doubts and frustrations.

As we ask these questions, we also might take time to consider how we make internal space to address the veil ourselves, with God's help. After all, we can be quite busy, and our calendars and lists often distract us. We have families to care for and careers to maintain. We have to run kids to activities and may have responsibilities to other groups ourselves. Even church activities have the potential to distract us. As if all of that wasn't enough, we still have basic household upkeep to manage: taking out the trash, washing dishes, mowing the lawn, and doing laundry. How, then, in the bustle of a typical day, does this work? How do we lift the veil?

Brother Lawrence was a Carmelite monk who lived in Paris in the seventeenth century. He is not really known for any grand speeches, writings, or miracles, but instead something much more subtle: he wrote a brief classic work called *The Practice of the Presence of God*, in which he shares how he takes time to notice God in his daily chores around the monastery. Whether while sweeping the floor, doing the dishes, or answering the need of a fellow monk, he could sense God in these ordinary acts as much as if he was receiving the bread and wine during Mass.[3]

No matter what he did throughout the day, Brother Lawrence imagined himself in constant conversation and communion with God. He noted that one's motive should not be the seeking of a pleasurable holy feeling, as that will not always happen. Instead, we may converse with God at all times because we know God loves us and would receive both this communication and our very selves with grace.[4]

Brother Lawrence's suggestion would seem to fit with a busy life, or a temperament that finds it hard to sit still for too long. Just as he did, we may be in conversation with God while walking the dog, rocking an infant, taking a shower, or cleaning the basement. God is already there anyway, so perhaps God has something to say to us. Intentional awareness and practice transforms how we see these activities and helps lift the veil.

The previous chapter began with an in-depth exploration of my dislike of winter and the frozen precipitation that it brings. By happenstance, this chapter takes us to a time of year as far away from that season as one can get. Once it becomes certain that we're clear of dealing with snow and ice; the last frost has come and gone, the snowblower can be tucked away in the garage in favor of the lawnmower, the trees and flowers begin to blossom and the temperature rises, I am able to turn my thoughts and attention to a variety of activities that the warmer weather of late spring and summer allow. By far, my favorite is wheeling the grill out to our patio and firing it up for the first time.

I barely exaggerate when I share that we live off of our grill during the warm half of the year. Many evenings, I forego the stove and microwave in favor of preparing many of our meals over an open flame: hot dogs, hamburgers, brats, kabobs, chicken, fish, and steaks. Our main courses this time of year often feature char marks and the faint taste of smoke enriched by the juices that have run off to make the fire burn higher and brighter.

Over the years, I've come to view grilling not just as an exercise in cooking, but as an entire experience. I love everything about it: the unique smells of the food as it is prepared; the sounds of sizzling and popping. I like the chance to be outside and observe the life growing around me as I take in the shade of the trees, the rays of the sun, and the birds overhead scouring the earth for food of their own. I love the creative art that is cooking itself: the experimentation with spice combinations and monitoring the selection of the evening to determine when it's ready. I love the sense of wider community that grilling sometimes brings; those opportunities for sharing this food not just with my immediate family, but with guests who have joined us for a meal, whether for a special occasion or just for the sake of enjoying one another's company for an evening.

Back in chapter 2, I explored how anything can be sacramental. Every moment of our day can be understood to convey God's presence and grace to us. For me, grilling has become one such practice where I am a little more aware of our world's divine underpinnings. I am able to slow down, observe creation around me and engage in a creative act myself. I am preparing something that will bring loved ones together around a common table and meal; an expression of relationship and a sharing of our lives with each other. God is in the creation and creating, in the relationships and in the sharing. And all of these opportunities to notice God's self-giving grace begins with a little propane and a spark.

And so it can be with any such activity. The simplest task can be an invitation to experience God with us. Through listening prayer, we open ourselves to God's self-communication, which in turn increases our sensitivity to how God shows up at times beyond prayerful reflection and our chosen spiritual discipline. Contemplation begins intentionally with scripture, art, or other materials, but as we develop new and holy habits, our objects of contemplation expand to include the entire world and all that we experience in it.

Coffeehouse Contemplative

A young woman with whom I met for spiritual direction came in to one of our sessions seeming especially encouraged by something she'd experienced during her most recent week of prayer. As a pharmacy technician, she often would have to deal with customers with poor attitudes. While she would deal with such people with the most cordial and professional manner she could muster, it would nevertheless require decompressing after the fact, and some days would leave her drained.

On the day of this session, she was excited to share an interaction with one such agitated man seeking to fill a prescription. She reflected, "Normally, I would let a person like this frustrate me and I'd think about all the things I want to say back to him but can't. This time, though, I was inspired to consider what he might be going through, what else might have happened in his day, that caused him to be so angry." Her daily prayer had changed her attitude toward someone with whom she'd normally be upset. She was able to approach him in a more contemplative manner, noting that there was more to the encounter that she couldn't see. She could remember that this other person was God's beloved creation, and this changed her way of seeing and interacting with him.

Contemplation is not just for clergy and members of religious orders, and it doesn't just happen in churches and monasteries. Through dedicated prayer and consideration, anyone is capable of becoming contemplative in coffeehouses, kitchens, pharmacies, the morning commute, hospital waiting rooms, and even the DMV. A regular practice cultivates within us a greater awareness of God wherever we are and in whatever we are doing.

As with anything related to our spiritual development, such an awareness takes time. God's gift of grace is one that unfolds to us at its own pace, and it may take our entire lives to explore its depth, meaning, and application. As with any relationship, we are always discovering how to best communicate our thoughts and feelings to even our closest loved ones, and they to us. Likewise, discerning God's self-communication is dependent on our receptiveness to it. Grace takes a while to blossom within us through careful nurture.[5]

Not only must one be patient in nurturing this awareness, but it is usually beneficial to do it alongside someone else. One of the primary purposes of spiritual direction is to identify how God is moving and communicating in the life of the one seeking it. This includes family, career, yard work, vacation, friendships, and all else that influences the particulars and complexity of one's sense of being. We often may not be able to see all the ways God knows us and searches us. Having another listen to our story often helps us see what we can't on our own.

Contemplation in daily life is something into which we grow. As the writer of 1 Peter describes it, we begin with "the pure, spiritual milk, so that by it you may grow into salvation" (1 Peter 2:2). We don't begin as seasoned experts. Instead, fostering a new spiritual consciousness takes much prayer, time, and attention.

Questions for Reflection

1. What experiences have you had lately where you wondered how God was a part of it? Is it easier to look back after the fact to see more clearly?

2. Reflect on the images of God that are most helpful to you. In light of those images, in what ways might the idea of God always searching and knowing you be comforting? Is there something about this idea that is troubling, or upsetting?

3. Consider Brother Lawrence's suggestion that we can experience God just as deeply while sweeping the floor as when we might be receiving communion. Why do you think God might be interested even in the small tasks that make up our days? What do you think that says about God's regard for you?

4. Over the next seven days, choose an activity that you do every day, or nearly so. Try to intentionally talk to God as you do it. By the end of the week, do you notice a difference in how you approach it, or how you see other aspects of your life?

Chapter 7

Grace in Dry Places

My junior year of college was a memorable time for me, largely for all the wrong reasons. Many may consider the college experience right below high school in terms of the amount of superficiality and self-centeredness that it involves. My late teen and early twenties years were not without their share of insulation and drama, and my junior year in particular featured enough to account for the entire four years that I spent at Heidelberg University in the small town of Tiffin, Ohio.

I must add, however, that while the typical college experience can be one of exploring (and exploiting) one's newfound independence, it can also be a time of incredible development, discovery, and self-actualization. It is, after all, the proverbial time of leaving the nest and learning to fly. And while that learning is happening, there are bound to be a few crashes.

I was involved in several campus ministry organizations at Heidelberg, one based on the ethos of the United Church of Christ (Heidelberg is affiliated with the UCC), and one loosely tied to a more evangelical parachurch organization that has a presence on many college campuses. For the first two years of my college career, I found both meaningful for different reasons. The UCC group helped me through some hard faith questions resultant from my religion coursework, and I loved the energy and expressiveness of the evangelical group. Both helped me explore new horizons and depths of spiritual formation, and to this day I am thankful for the part that both played in my journey during those years.

My junior year, however, brought about a series of personal shifts that could have been more manageable if they'd come one at a time. Unfortunately, we can't choose the way these events happen, and so I had to deal with several at once instead.

My relationship with the evangelical group began to change during this year. I began voicing my disagreement with chosen tactics of evangelism that I saw as more damaging than helpful, and I also began questioning some of the theological positions of others in this ministry. I had been forceful enough about these issues over a long enough period of time that I sensed some friendships beginning to deteriorate, and my role in the ministry beginning to shift to one of outsider. What made this especially difficult was the indirect nature of this change: seldom did a conversation happen between me and others, but comments and gossip eventually found their way back to me. To some, I had "strayed from the path," despite my best explanations to the contrary and attempts to appeal to common ground.

In hindsight, part of this was my acting out of a new round of doubts and questions that had emerged within me, although one much more serious than the season through which the UCC group had journeyed with me two years earlier. This latest crisis, the result of discovering new writing and scholarship questioning the veracity of Jesus' life and compounded by an eroding base of support, left me in a spiritually weakened state, to the point where I couldn't bring myself even to pray for help. No amount of comforting scriptures, or forcing myself to continue attending worship and other faith-related activities, seemed to bring relief to the doubts churning inside of me. It certainly didn't help to see certain people at many of these functions whose friendship and trust was no longer available during a time when it was sorely needed.

Finally, one evening, I found myself on the floor of a dorm hallway with a thin NIV Bible. My then-girlfriend had settled down in bed for the night, and for some reason I'd decided to linger outside her room. On the verge of giving up completely, I stared at this small book as if it was my final leatherette-bound shred of hope. My faith was in shambles, as were many relationships on which I'd previously relied, and was looking into a future with far more uncertainty than before. Up until this point, I knew that I was here to major in religion, and I knew that I was going to seminary, and I knew that I was going to become a pastor. But in the face of incredible doubt both of God and of myself, I was much less sure that I knew much of anything.

For the first time in months, I managed the tiniest of prayers: "Please show me something." Even those four words were quite the accomplishment in that particular moment. Flipping open the book on my lap, my eyes fell on Luke 24:34: "It is true! The Lord has risen, and has appeared to Simon!" (NIV) The feeling of relief that washed over me upon discovering that verse, which I believe to be Spirit-guided, is hard to quantify with words even all these years later. But I can describe how well I slept that night, reassured that something larger than me was still watching, guiding, listening, even suffering alongside me.

I'll be the first to tell you that flipping open a Bible doesn't always yield the results that it did for me that night. But for that moment, at least, God made God's presence known on the musty, tamped-down carpet of a dorm hallway to a 20-year-old kid desperately praying for a lifeline after months of flailing about in a sea of despair. I've already reflected on God being in coffeehouses and in doing the dishes; God could be here, too. I still credit that night of answered desperation with renewing my sense of call and self. It hadn't removed the hardships I was facing, but it did provide some much-needed spiritual fortitude to keep moving forward.

Sitting in the Dust

So far we have described how close God is to us; how God is ever pursuing relationship with us through a gracious gift of God's own presence. I have also encouraged you, my reader, to seek out this presence; to nurture it intentionally for a deepened awareness of God's inspiring and transforming forgiveness. One inevitable and understandable question may arise: *what about those times when God seems silent, absent, or uncaring?*

The list of occasions that may give rise to this question is long and varied. As in my story above, it may come during a time of intense doubt or eroding social support. It may come while struggling with physical or mental illness. It may come with loss of a job, home, or loved one. It may come during any season of life when our sense of stability and normalcy is thrown into chaos.

With these times comes a more urgent need for reassurance that God is still in relationship with us, close to us in our times of greatest suffering and anxiety. *How is God with us in these hours of need? Is God present at all?* These questions have haunted people of faith since humanity first developed a capacity for spiritual awareness. Where is God in times of doubt, pain, disaster, despair, and loss?

A common answer that many offer is that God is the cause of such events. This answer is rooted in a theology that God is in control, working toward a grand finale that is beyond any demand for God's self-justification in the short-term aftermath. God is free from scrutiny in this view because God out of divine sovereignty doesn't actually owe us an explanation. Tragedies like cancer, earthquakes, droughts, mental disorders, and stillbirths are simply part of an unspoken plan that on a long enough time line will help reveal God's power and goodness to the world.

A second answer commonly offered is that such things happen because the person enduring them was sinful enough to warrant it. God is present via punishment and discipline, urging us toward repentance and renewed commitment to God's will. This is the explanation offered by Job's friends while he sits in the dust of the ground, having lost all that he holds dear including his family. They keep encouraging him to confess to God what he has done to deserve such suffering, and that is what will alleviate his pain. This comes after the single helpful thing these visitors do, which is just to sit silently with him for the first seven days of their visit (Job 2:13).

Each of these explanations suggest that God is present in tragedy as its cause. They are meant to provide assurance that God is in complete control of what is happening, and has a plan to redeem the person experiencing it. Each of these explanations also has great potential to be spiritually damaging.

The first explanation presents an image of God who enacts tragedy for God's own sake, rather than for the sake of, much less love of, God's creation. This view encourages us to believe that all will be revealed and that we must continue giving God our trust despite God inflicting natural disasters, life-threatening health crises, sudden loss of loved ones, and critical faith questions upon us. Relationships in which one causes pain to another while expecting persistent devotion are categorized as abusive; insisting that we remain with a God who treats us this way while demanding our love is abusive spirituality. This type of divine image leads many people to reject God, rather than draw closer to God.

The second explanation—that of suffering as punishment—does not seem to reveal a God of transformative forgiveness as incarnate in Jesus. Rather than begin with grace, it sets up the one experiencing loss to be on a constant quest for God's approval in the hope that if he or she just does a little more, God will relent from the harm that God has caused. This view not only results in an image of God whose primary characteristics are anger, coercion, and retribution, but also in an image of self where I must work to become indefinitely more lovable because God finds who I am now not to be good enough. This helps perpetuate the mask of the false self (as discussed in chapter 3).

In the Gospels, we meet a Jesus who heals diseases, welcomes the outsider, restores those considered sinful and unclean, weeps at a friend's tomb, and corrects those who say that tragedy is caused by sin. He shows people a God concerned with suffering enough to become an imminent and intimate participant in it alongside others. He reveals a God who has forgiven first, rather than making the reduction of pain conditional upon consciously receiving it. He rarely offers simple answers to life's harshness, but instead walks, touches, welcomes, and says, "do not be afraid."

Jesus shows us a different way to think about how God is with us while we sit in the dust of despair, uncertainty, and grief. He reveals a God who does not cause our pain, but rather journeys with us through our pain; our suffering as beloved creatures matters to our Creator. Karl Rahner states that God does this freely in Jesus, completely subjecting God's self to human history and all that comes with it. God chooses to do this above other options—including aloofly causing pain for self-glorification—and for this reason scripture declares God and love to be synonymous.[1]

As Rahner repeatedly suggests, God's very presence is how God shares grace with us. The Incarnation most completely reveals this, as Jesus embodies this gift by taking on both humanity's joy and sorrow.[2] How, then, might we think about this gift at times when we doubt that it is really there?

Finding Consolation in Desolate Times

> *Surely the Lord your God has blessed you in all your undertakings; he knows your going through this great wilderness. These forty years the Lord your God has been with you; you have lacked nothing.* (Deuteronomy 2:7)

> *And the Spirit immediately drove him out into the wilderness. He was in the wilderness forty days, tempted by Satan; and he was with the wild beasts; and the angels waited on him.* (Mark 1:12–13)

The Hebrew and Christian scriptures sometimes use the imagery or setting of wilderness. After their liberation from Egypt, the

Israelites spend 40 years in the wilderness before entering the land of Canaan. After his baptism, Jesus spends 40 days in the wilderness before beginning his public ministry. Each of these narratives offer an idea of what the wilderness is like: it is outside the comforts of civilization, features unknown dangers, lacks sustaining resources, and causes the person wandering through it to at least entertain the notion of going back to former ways of life because they featured something that was recognizable and at least provided the illusion of safety.

Wilderness-wandering is characterized by scarcity. In the wilderness, the abundance of something in which we used to take comfort is no longer apparent, or it no longer brings the same relief and certainty that it had before. Many situations may push us into a spiritual wilderness, where those resources that previously sustained us no longer do so. We are in a new, unfamiliar, dry landscape where we crave an assurance of God's presence and we cry out for relief and renewal.

Ignatius of Loyola fittingly calls these moments of doubt and despair spiritual desolation. While in this state, Ignatius writes, we find ourselves struggling with disquiet and agitation of the soul; feelings of disturbance and sorrow. These feelings tend to lead to a lack of confidence in the presence of hope and love: we find ourselves sapped of our energy, unable to participate in spiritual practices we found meaningful before, as if we are cut off from God completely.[3] Our most dominant and intrusive thoughts in times of desolation cause us to consider giving up on God and on ourselves. We may find little solace in our usual coping mechanisms and spiritual resources during these periods.

Ignatius offers a few important reminders for while we are enduring a season of desolation. First, he notes that it is important not to make any monumental life-changing decisions. We may be prone to believing that our usual routines, relationships, or environment are the cause of our spiritual drought; that a shift in one or more of these areas of our lives will help break its hold on us. Our human nature often wishes for quick fixes and easy answers, which such a change would be more often than not. This tactic may provide a false hope, a mirage in the desert, rather than a true, lasting solution.

Instead, it may be best to hold fast to practices and resources that we had found reliable before desolation, and in turn pay greater attention to prayer activities, seeking counsel with a spiritual director or mentor, and observing healthy self-care. When we are in this state, we should seek out ways to remind ourselves of God's faithfulness and love for us.[4] Even if what we had found meaningful before doesn't seem productive in our current spiritual season, a continued faithful attentiveness may still be what helps us find our footing.

In times of desolation, consider that God is not the cause. Contrary to explanations critiqued earlier in the chapter, God does not bring desolation on us to prove God's goodness or to punish us. However, God may use these times; working through them to strengthen our faith and to teach us more about God's love and about ourselves. Our relationship with God and our ability to discern God's presence and grace develop and expand and deepen during these times, much more so than they would if we always managed to feel comfortable and secure.[5] The circumstances themselves are not a gift from God, but God still gifts us with God's grace even while more difficult to discern in times of hardship.

Returning again to my own faith story, the causes of my season of desolation were multiple. They involved both relationships around me and doubts within me. I lost confidence both in God's presence and activity in my life, as well as in my sense of identity and purpose. I never felt as if God was inflicting this on me, but rather questioned where God was as these interior movements wreaked havoc on my spirit. I did find, however, that I couldn't easily give up certain practices such as attending group fellowship activities. There was still something about showing up that seemed important; that I needed. When I couldn't pray myself, I asked others to pray for me; to lift up words on my behalf while I listened in silent longing. The night that I sat in that hallway, I turned to something that before my faith crisis occurred had been sure and steadfast: the scriptures that I treasured studying and learning about.

Any spiritual journey will feature times in the desert, when there seems to be nothing to do but sit down in the dust and wonder where God is. It helps to store up memories of God's presence and activity for these parts of the journey, as they will help restore our parched spirits and remind us that God's ability to bring new life out of worn out and broken things is still true.

Desolation in the Psalms

The book of Psalms is a unique gift to those who claim it as part of their faith text. While all books of the Hebrew scriptures and New Testament give special insight into how individuals and groups discerned God's work among them, the poetry of this book, written from the point of view of an individual or on behalf of the gathered worshiping community, spans the entire spectrum of human emotion and experience as the writer celebrates God's blessing in times of prosperity and peace, or wrestles with God's perceived absence in times of upheaval, loss, and doubt.

The Psalms regularly express spiritual desolation. At times the writer may praise God for the many ways he and his people have experienced God's love and faithfulness. At other times, he may express anger or frustration at God for seemingly leaving him to fend for himself in the face of oppression, loneliness, and deep questioning. In these latter psalms, the writer hardly ever minces words or pulls punches. He doesn't have time to dress up his petitions and concerns in the reverent language to which we may be accustomed. In these psalms, the writer's situation is too urgent to make his prayers sound nice.

Biblical scholar Walter Brueggemann suggests that the use of these psalms that express anger and doubt are actually acts of bold faith for two reasons. First, such psalms acknowledge the world's harshness and engage it as it is rather than under pretense. Second, such psalms insist that all life experiences, including those of chaos and disorientation, are within the bounds of what people of faith can address with God.[6] I call the book of Psalms a gift among the scriptures because they show that this same permission to bring all of life's particularities and predicaments to God is afforded to us as well. They show that we are allowed to lament, question, and rant to God about our own deeply-felt heartaches and longings.

Psalm 22 is one such example of a psalm written in a time of anger and doubt:

> *My God, my God, why have you forsaken me?*
> *Why are you so far from helping me, from the words of my groaning?*
> *O my God, I cry by day, but you do not answer;*
> *and by night, but find no rest.*
> *Yet you are holy,*
> *enthroned on the praises of Israel.*
> *In you our ancestors trusted;*
> *they trusted, and you delivered them.*
> *To you they cried, and were saved;*
> *in you they trusted, and were not put to shame.*
> *But I am a worm, and not human;*
> *scorned by others, and despised by the people.*
> *All who see me mock at me;*
> *they make mouths at me, they shake their heads;*
> *"Commit your cause to the Lord; let him deliver—*
> *let him rescue the one in whom he delights!"*
> *Yet it was you who took me from the womb;*
> *you kept me safe on my mother's breast.*

On you I was cast from my birth,
and since my mother bore me you have been my God.
Do not be far from me,
for trouble is near
and there is no one to help.
Many bulls encircle me,
strong bulls of Bashan surround me;
they open wide their mouths at me,
like a ravening and roaring lion.
am poured out like water,
and all my bones are out of joint;
my heart is like wax;
it is melted within my breast;
my mouth is dried up like a potsherd,
and my tongue sticks to my jaws;
you lay me in the dust of death.
For dogs are all around me;
a company of evildoers encircles me.
My hands and feet have shriveled;
I can count all my bones.
They stare and gloat over me;
they divide my clothes among themselves,
and for my clothing they cast lots.
But you, O Lord, do not be far away!
O my help, come quickly to my aid!
Deliver my soul from the sword,
my life from the power of the dog!
Save me from the mouth of the lion!
From the horns of the wild oxen
you have rescued me.
I will tell of your name to my brothers and sisters;
in the midst of the congregation I will praise you:
You who fear the Lord, praise him!

All you offspring of Jacob, glorify him;
stand in awe of him, all you offspring of Israel!
For he did not despise or abhor
the affliction of the afflicted;
he did not hide his face from me,
but heard when I cried to him.
From you comes my praise in the great congregation;
my vows I will pay before those who fear him.
The poor shall eat and be satisfied;
those who seek him shall praise the Lord.
May your hearts live forever!
All the ends of the earth shall remember
and turn to the Lord;
and all the families of the nations
shall worship before him.
For dominion belongs to the L ORD ,
and he rules over the nations.
To him, indeed, shall all who
sleep in the earth bow down;
before him shall bow all who go down to the dust,
and I shall live for him.
Posterity will serve him; future generations will be told
about the Lord,
and proclaim his deliverance to a people yet unborn,
saying that he has done it (NRSV).

The first two verses help set the tone: "My God, my God, why have you forsaken me? Why are you so far from helping me, from the words of my groaning? O my God, I cry by day, but you do not answer; and by night, but find no rest." (Psalm 22:1–2) Here the writer gets right to the point, without taking the time to dress up what he wants to say. He is crying out for, even demanding, an account of God's whereabouts in a time of despair. These verses may be familiar to Christians as some of the final words that Jesus utters from the cross in Matthew and Mark. Such an appearance in that account illustrates the psalm's universal application: it speaks to an experience that transcends any particular set of circumstances. It assists people of faith with finding language for times of suffering and need.[7]

The writer continues to express his doubt later in the psalm, using a diversity of metaphors for what he is feeling. His heart is melted like wax within his chest (22:14), and his mouth is dry like a potsherd (22:15). This theme of dryness is recurring, as he describes his tongue sticking to his jaws and lying in dust. It is a desolate time for the psalmist, and he is being forthright with God about his dryness of spirit.

Intertwined with these expressions of desolation, however, are words of faith and hope. After those opening exclamations of lament, he is quick to remember the stories of God delivering his ancestors from oppression and harm: "to you they cried, and were saved; in you they trusted, and were not put to shame" (22:5). Later, his faith confession takes a more personal tone: "since my mother bore me you have been my God" (22:10). In these verses, the psalmist appeals to spiritual sources on which he has relied in the past, returning to these inner shrines to remember that though his circumstances have changed, God's presence and faithfulness have not. The final 10 verses of this psalm are a full-blown expression of praise and thanksgiving for God's provision for those in need, hearing of all those who call.

There is some indication that the latter part of this psalm is due to the writer's own situation resolving, but he also acknowledges God as his perpetual source of strength even along spiritually dry paths. He gives voice to his own season of desolation, but even interwoven with it are times of provision and assurance remembered and newly experienced; spiritual oases from which he may drink and give relief to parched lips straining to utter prayers.

The psalmist's spiritual journey may be anyone's. He could have written of feeling forsaken by God sitting next to a parent's hospital bed. He could have written about his heart melting while signing divorce papers or waiting for a child to come out of surgery. He could have written about sitting in the dust of death by the grave of a friend gone at too young an age. These are but a few of the many instances that may unsettle our faith; that may throw our spirits into a time of desolation.

And yet the psalmist is also resolute in remembering who God has been for him. He recalls the narratives handed down that he has made his own. He remembers the ways he has been nurtured by stories, songs, and practices prior to his present difficulties. He dips into these stored-up consolations in the hope and trust that God is still with him; that his awareness of God has changed, but what was true in times of prosperity is still true in discord because he knows that these latter times are when it needs to be the most.

Psalms for a New Day

Christian spirituality has a rich well of scripture, songs, poetry, prose, and art from which to draw when traveling through spiritually dry places. The writer of Psalm 22 gives voice to a desolate experience in such a way that we may be able to hear our own in his words. Using these psalms of lament as a focus of meditation described previously could be one fruitful practice in our own times of desolation.

Another helpful practice might be to try writing an original psalm more personal to the individual or immediate community. This sort of spiritual exercise may help us to understand our interior movements—those emotions and thoughts churning inside of us that we may not understand until we take time to sort through them—to name what they are and to process their meaning in order to discern a path forward with God's guidance.

Several things are important to remember when sitting down for such an exercise. First, like the psalmists of old, we have permission to be honest about what we are feeling and our longing for a greater awareness of God's presence. Through the incarnation, Jesus shows us a God intimately involved in the human experience, including times of anger, sadness, and uncertainty. These emotions are fair subject matter for prayerful engagement.

The second thing to remember is to draw from past consolations not only to find sustenance and encouragement for this new moment of desolation, but also as a resource for making sense of it. The writer of Psalm 22 is up front with his questions and sense of despair and loneliness, but also mentions who he has known God to be in calmer, more fulfilling moments.

Here again is where spiritual direction may be a helpful resource, both in the naming of our own interior movements in order to put them to words, but also in the exploration of what we end up writing. We may also need direction for reminders of the ways we have been nurtured in times past before our present season in the wilderness, encouragement to remain steadfast in practices we previously found helpful, and to have someone willing to pray for us when we cannot pray for ourselves.

Our own desolation psalms can serve as highly personal insights into our own spirits, as well as deepen our awareness of God as more than a good feeling when things are going well. The simple act of asking our questions or expressing our fears may help us begin to find God again, struggling and weeping with us. Exploring and naming the causes and effects of our desolations may be the beginning of consolation.

Questions for Reflection

1. Can you name times in your life where feelings of spiritual desolation or consolation were especially notable? What was happening in your life at that time?

2. In times of spiritual desolation, what practices, people, or resources have been your greatest aids in sorting through it? How were they helpful?

3. Read through the entirety of Psalm 22. What experiences of your own do you hear in the writer's words? How have you drawn from times of consolation when dealing with times of desolation?

4. Try sitting down to write your own psalm, whether you are in a time of consolation or desolation. Include elements such as how you think God is with you, or how you have experienced God in the past to help give perspective for a spiritually dry time. What new insights does writing to God in this way produce?

Chapter 8

Encountering Together

Hopefully you don't put the book down after you finish reading this sentence: *I'm a Michigan football fan*. I was born in Southfield, a north suburb of Detroit, and spent the first eight years of my life in various communities around the state. My father was a pastor, and multiple moves within the span of a decade are a featured element of the lifestyle for many clergy families. Thanks both to my living in the state for that stretch of time along with my paternal grandfather having attended the university for a few years, I had a love for the colors maize and blue ingrained into me beginning at a very early age. I grew up learning the players, coaches, fight song, and battle cry of what remains to this day my favorite team in any sport.

When I was in second grade, my family moved once again, this time further south to northeast Ohio, where I learned very quickly that not very many people in my new surroundings are very fond of the so-called Team Up North. Fortunately for me, the late 1980s and most of the 90s were pleasant times in the Michigan/Ohio State rivalry: I could show up to school most years after what fans on both sides simply call The Game with my head high and nary a word from the downcast faces of my scarlet and grey classmates.

This all took a turn in the new century, when a series of moves on both sides began to cause a lag in Michigan's fortunes, and the program started to fall behind. Since the year 2000, the Wolverines have suffered the first loss ever to a team from a lower division, multiple losing seasons, the loss of many long-standing team records and streaks, and several overhauls to the coaching staff. All of this would have been difficult to bear regardless of my place of residence, but that this valley of fandom occurred while I live in rival territory has added an extra layer to the misery.

My brother and I make a pilgrimage up to Ann Arbor at least one fall Saturday every season to attend a game. We usually meet up early in the morning in full fan gear to make the drive. Once we arrive in town, we explore the area close to the stadium, enjoy lunch at a local restaurant, and wander through the tailgates. The colors and logos of the team—my team—surround us in abundance. I walk around freely and without fear of ridicule or remark. Once at my seat, the fight song rings out from someplace deep in my lungs, and every touchdown brings me to my feet along with over a hundred thousand others, while every misstep causes us to release a collective groan of disappointment. For one day a year, sports-wise, I am among my people, all of us together for the singular purpose of cheering for our guys on the field. And I can commiserate with them in our mutual passion for a few hours, feeling affirmed and at ease, and my love renewed just by being around those who share it. For just a little while, I am among those with whom I can share an experience, as well as an interpretation of that experience, before heading back to my place of exile down south.

This is what happens in any sort of group, club, or community of which we're willingly a part: we come together in order to experience connection over something we hold in common. We may gather over interests and hobbies such as fantasy sports leagues, crafts, music, or wine-tasting. We may come together for support and to give voice to our struggle with grief, addiction, or mental illness. We gather in many cases just to be with others: whether over a meal, an afternoon in the park, or to wind down in a pub after a busy week, where we are together simply because relationships help us navigate the events of our days through story, laughter, tears, and the giving and receiving of love. Whether a close-knit group of a few or a large network of many, sharing in community serves as an invitation to process our experiences, challenge one another's thinking, commiserate in times of joy and sadness, and provide a fundamental assurance that we are not alone even when the world around us causes us to feel as if we are.

Like my annual trip to Ann Arbor, sharing in community enriches our experience of everyday life as we indulge in and react to it alongside others. We remember that even if we can't see those who make up our closest and most trusted relationships as often as we like, we nonetheless remain connected. And before long, we may be able to reconnect in order to listen and to be heard; to empathize in pleasure and pain, to offer or be offered a perspective not yet considered, to be refreshed and affirmed before rejoining a reality that we may find hostile or harsh. Community draws us into a life of mutuality, support, and growth that we can't achieve on our own.

Called into Spiritual Community

Many may assume that Christian spiritual practices are for observance in solitude. When we speak of a "personal spirituality," we are indeed speaking about one's own relationship to God; how each individual senses God in one's own life, how his or her images of God are constructive or damaging, and how one's discernment of God affects one's sense of self. As such, spiritual practices do call us to examine ourselves in light of how we sense that God is with us. However, as I have noted in previous chapters, our images of God and self do not arise by sole virtue of our own observation, insight, and reflection. These images involve many influences including our family of origin, any religious tradition in which we were raised, the wider culture in which we live, and the peer groups in which we participate.

We're already members of a series of intersecting communities, some of which we treasure more than others, that have had an effect on how we view God and ourselves, as well as how we relate those to each other. Our spirituality is personal in the sense that it is our own and is unique to us, but it has developed as the result of many other factors, including the communities of which we're a part.

When we come to a point where we want to intentionally consider these images; what they mean to us and whether or not they are helpful, as well as nurture existing or new images through prayer and other disciplines, doing so in community is beneficial—essential, even—to that effort. When we are able to locate a spiritual community that we can trust, we are able to come together around a common set of beliefs and practices to encourage one another, hear one another's experiences, offer new perspectives on those experiences, and regularly check in to see if each member is remaining faithful to the spiritual disciplines each has undertaken. An entire community can offer spiritual direction to one another, so long as each has covenanted to be intentional about these things on an ongoing basis.

The word for community perhaps most familiar to those nurturing their spirituality in a Christian tradition is "church." However, this word may carry a lot of baggage for people, whether one is a committed part of such a community, is teetering on the outskirts wondering whether to continue, or has long given up on church as it is typically conceived in American society. It will be worthwhile, then, to spend some time considering and reclaiming this word in order to explore how being part of a church is still a useful undertaking for spirituality.

As with the word "religious" or "religion," the word "church" may conjure images of an institution of brick, mortar, steeple, and stained glass, with expectations both stated and implied. For an increasing number of people, this idea of church is spiritually stifling: as generational approaches to gathering in community have changed, younger people in particular feel less of a need to join formal groups and clubs—including the neighborhood church—the way their parents and grandparents did. Groups like the "spiritual but not religious" discussed in chapter 2 may question the need for driving to a building once a week, let alone a number of times, in order to nurture one's sense of connection to God and self.

Those who consider themselves regular and devoted members may also have particular ideas of what constitutes church. When most people talk about "going to church," for instance, they usually mean the Sunday morning worship event. That regular time spent with a majority of other regular attendees is the most visible form of the church. People hardly ever use the phrase "going to church" to refer to the Tuesday committee meeting, the Thursday Bible study, or the Saturday service project. For most, church means Sunday morning, and those other events go by other names.

The origin of the word "church" comes from the Greek *ekklesia*, which means "gathering" or "assembly." It is a combination of the Greek words for "out" and "to call."[1] So the word "church" literally means to be called out into a time of gathering together. At its root, to be part of a church is to gather with others; to be in community with fellow believers. Referring to Sunday worship as church is technically correct, as it is a gathered assembly of people, the most visible such gathering that a typical institution observes. But naming the committee meeting, Bible study, and service project as church would also be accurate, as each of these features believers assembled together, albeit in smaller numbers and for different purposes.

While at its heart church is a gathering of believers, many theologians and denominations have declared that there are other features of such gatherings that specifically mark them as a church. For instance, one of the forefathers of my own denominational tradition, John Calvin, stated that the presence of faithful preaching and the administration of the sacraments are what designate a gathering as a church.[2] Others may argue that the adherence to certain doctrinal statements, the necessity of baptism, or other particular practices make a church what it is. While these definitions are flexible enough so as not to necessitate the use of a building with certain features—preaching and sacraments could take place in a basement, restaurant, or someone's backyard—they still may limit gatherings to certain practices and not others, and such gatherings like a Bible study or mission trip may have another focus, but no less constitute church due to its basic nature as an assembly of the faithful gathered to experience God's presence faithfully spoken to and embodied for one another, which at their fundamental level is what preaching and the sacraments are meant to do.

All of this is to say that being in community with others for the sake of spiritual enrichment doesn't necessarily mean attending or joining a church, at least as it is commonly perceived in its institutional form. For some, particularly those inextricably wounded by such places, this is no longer an option. Many churches in the United Church of Christ and in other denominations strive to be places of healing for such wounds, but not everyone will see crossing the threshold even of these spaces as a viable possibility. It may be that a different way of gathering, of being the church, is necessary.

The Case for Gathering At All

As a pastor, I regularly read and hear the stories of people who have left the institutional version of church behind. I find it important to pay attention to these voices not to woo them back, but because I believe they help keep us honest. People still involved with traditional forms of church are in constant danger of developing tunnel vision, where considering the perspective of those outside its walls becomes difficult. Without attempting to be exhaustive, some of the more common reasons why people leave churches that I've heard over the years include feeling excluded or shunned, disagreement with the church's worldview or how it expresses that worldview to others, a lack of engagement with social justice issues, and placing the institution above individual or group concerns.

Many with whom I've spoken have attempted to connect with other churches, willing to believe that perhaps the issues they're trying to leave behind will not manifest elsewhere. Some find success in this while others do not, and the latter group eventually gives up the search entirely, burned out on trying to find a formal faith community in which they feel welcomed, connected, and engaged. These are not the "church shoppers" maligned in many places who seek out the most benefits and creature comforts they can find, but devoted believers wanting to express wonder, ask questions, engage in service, and feel like their involvement is valued. The search becomes tiresome after enough attempts, and many come to the conclusion that it might be better to explore other options for spiritual growth.

At times when listening to these stories, the one sharing it may ask, "Why search for spiritual community at all?" This may include not only traditional churches, but less formal gatherings as well. Why pursue community in any form? Why can't I simply practice meditative prayer and grow closer to God on my own, without checking in with a larger group in some way? These sorts of questions are understandable from those who have experienced spiritual community as unwelcoming, discouraging of questions, and protective of assets over people. After so many false starts, why keep trying?

As I have already explored, community of any kind serves a variety of purposes, the most basic being assurance that we may share our experiences with another. As with my annual journey to Michigan Stadium, community may provide an opportunity to share in a common interest or passion, and a space to process experiences of that interest or passion while listening to perspectives different from our own. I may have certain opinions about a play that didn't go well, but the fellow fan siting next to me might explain why the coach might have chosen it or why it went poorly. An older fan who has always lived in Michigan and who perhaps attended the university could share what it has been like coming to games for so long, while I could tell him about what it's like to live out of state and look forward to this single trip every fall. A younger fan attending for the first time might ask me about gameday traditions: what we do and when, as well as why we do them. We build common reference points through teaching one another the history of the program and the common language we use when discussing the game, the team, songs, and cheers. Each of us could obtain this information on our own through self-study, but we are instead participating in a moment, enhancing one another's experience of it in a way that researching questions even mere hours after the fact could not.

Karl Rahner suggests that our interior processing of our social and historical reality requires shared interpretation. We each strive to make sense of daily events both monumental and mundane, but such meaning-making is subjective to our own lenses and filters. We may not see something as clearly or glean significance from notable occurrences as objectively as we believe.[3]

Our spiritual experiences are our own; no one can take them away from us. As with my dorm hallway encounter shared in a previous chapter, if we believe we have had a genuine realization of God's presence, then that ultimately is ours to cherish and from which to draw strength and reassurance. At the same time, however, those with whom we share these personal revelations may help us interpret them, and we may end up seeing aspects we hadn't previously considered or gain a greater depth of appreciation for these moments than we could with our single viewpoint. In turn, others could also benefit from hearing about how we have seen God at work in our lives in order for them to ponder ways God has manifested in their own. We suggest reference points from scripture or tradition to one another that may help give name to what we are describing. We may develop a shared theological vocabulary on which to build our understanding of our and each other's stories.

Spiritual community doesn't necessarily mean institutional church. But it does mean a gathering of mutual support, affirmation, and accountability in which we may participate in shared interpretation. We offer our own experiences both for our own benefit and for others, to pursue a deepened understanding of how God is with us and who God wants us to be, and to hear our encounters repeated back by different voices and perspectives. And we may offer that same gift to those with whom we are in relationship. Whether a traditional church setting or an informal get-together in one's home, an intentional gathering of this sort is based upon the common interest and passion of helping one another see God's self-giving grace at work a little more clearly than we could by ourselves.

The Needs of the Body

One of the better known metaphors for spiritual community in the New Testament appears in 1 Corinthians 12. One of Paul's primary concerns while composing this letter was what he saw as abuse or exploitation of the concept of God's grace. Multiple clues throughout the letter help us deduce that there were people among the believers in Corinth who saw grace as a license to do whatever they wanted. They argued that God has bestowed this gift of love, forgiveness, and presence without my having to do anything, and thus whatever I do is automatically covered. I can willfully do whatever I want, the reasoning goes, and if things get too bad, I can start again like getting another life in a video game.

Paul strongly pushes back against this highly self-focused rationalization. He argues against a disembodied voice that says, "All things are lawful:" "but not all things are beneficial," he snaps back (1 Cor. 10:23). The Corinthian believers are receptive to God's capacity to forgive, but they don't allow it to transform their outlook of themselves. They do not receive grace in a gracious manner. So Paul seeks to clarify the impact that this gift is meant to have on them as individuals and as a community.

For just as the body is one and has many members, and all the members of the body, though many are one body, so it is with Christ. For in the one Spirit we were all baptized into one body—Jews or Greeks, slaves or free—and we were all made to drink of one Spirit.

Indeed, the body does not consist of one member but of many. If the foot would say, "Because I am not a hand, I do not belong to the body," that would not make it any less a part of the body. And if the ear would say, "Because I am not an eye, I do not belong to the body," that would not make it any less a part of the body. If the whole body were an eye, where would the hearing be? If the whole body were hearing, where would the sense of smell be? But as it is, God arranged the members in the body, each one of them, as he chose. If all were a single member, where would the body be? As it is, there are many members, yet one body. The eye cannot say to the hand, "I have no need of you," nor again the head to the feet, "I have no need of you." On the contrary, the members of the body that seem to be weaker are indispensable, and those members of the body that we think less honorable we clothe with greater honor, and our less respectable members are treated with greater respect; whereas our more respectable members do not need this. But God has so arranged the body, giving the greater honor to the inferior member, that there may be no dissension within the body, but the members may have the same care for one another. If one member suffers, all suffer together with it; if one member is honored, all rejoice together with it (1 Corinthians 12:12–26 NRSV).

In this passage, Paul uses the analogy of a body to make a point about community: "Just as the body is one and has many members, and all the members of the body, though many, are one boy, so it is with Christ" (1 Cor. 12:12). This comes after a lengthy discussion of spiritual gifts, and how every member of the community has something to contribute.

Paul continues by explaining that every body part has its role to play, both from the perspective of each part and of the whole. "If the foot would say, 'Because I am not a hand, I do not belong to the body,' that would not make it any less a part of the body" (12:15). There are times, Paul acknowledges, when people do not feel very connected to the faith community. They may feel like they don't fit in; outcasts among what is supposed to be an affirming and inclusive place. If only I was something other than I am, one may dejectedly reason, maybe I would be accepted. This reasoning contributes to how we develop the mask of our false self.

And yet, God's self-giving presence is with everyone, regardless of the ways humanity tries to place limitations and restrictions upon it. God's reckless forgiveness easily side-steps our attempts to erect fences to contain it. Perhaps not every manifestation of the body will be the right fit for everyone, but we are nonetheless invited to find a gathering of people who will share in our spiritual journey without first demanding that we make ourselves acceptable.

Continuing with his metaphor, Paul then switches to the needs of the body: "The eye cannot say to the hand, 'I have no need of you,' nor again the head to the feet, 'I have no need of you'" (12:21). Every part of the body has a valued role to play, and in a community meant to share in God's self-giving presence together, the unique perspectives and backgrounds of each enriches the shared interpretation of the whole. A body that only gives attention to the information provided by eyesight, for instance, misses out on what the other senses can add to the experience.

Paul concludes this passage with what he believes to be the essence of unity as a body: "If one member suffers, all suffer together with it; if one member is honored, all rejoice together with it" (12:26). If a community approaches its identity and tasks seriously, it will strive to be a space of mutual engagement where each member is loved, respected, and affirmed. The shared interpretation around which we gather includes processing one another's stories with prayerful empathy and solidarity. Joy and suffering are inevitable features of the spiritual journey, even if they take different forms for each of us. The community's first task is to listen and to acknowledge it. The needs of each may determine how to interpret these experiences faithfully and with a sense of God's guidance, and always according to the gracious recognition that no one should have to walk their path alone.

Spiritual direction is based on the premise that we journey with one or more people in discerning where God is in our lives. Sometimes—perhaps more often than we think—listening to another's observations about our questions, encounters, doubts, concerns, triumphs, and daily tasks may reveal possibilities to us that we would not have considered if left to our own reflection.

And yet Ignatius of Loyola provides caution to the one guiding another through his Spiritual Exercises: get out of the way. In any form of spiritual direction, whether meeting one on one with a director or engaged in a community gathering, it is critical that one respect the spiritual journey of each as their own, allowing for God to deal directly with each person as much as possible.[4]

In a community setting, we may be tempted to direct another to come around to our own way of thinking or to try providing for someone else their own version of a divine encounter that we ourselves found meaningful. We may do this in conscious and subconscious ways, but it is a strong caution for anyone entrusted with helping another in shared interpretation.

A well-trained and self-aware spiritual director will strive to keep from doing this with his or her directees. They are guides along the path, helping you describe what you have seen while walking and helping you discern the options for what lies ahead. This is the spiritual community's work as well: allowing one's journey to be their own and giving thanks for how God is dealing directly with them, but helping to name what that work has been and could be as well.

As we have all found to be the case in our own way, being in community has its risks. But the rest of the body may alert us to grace in ways we wouldn't have noticed otherwise, and we each as valued and unique members may contribute what we have seen for another's benefit as well.

Questions for Reflection

1. Think of all the different communities of which you are currently a part. This may include support groups, groups formed around common interests or hobbies, or a core of friends that get together regularly. Try to name why they are special to you, and what they add to your identity as an individual.

2. Whether in a traditional church or an alternative gathering, what has been your experience of spiritual community, both positive and negative? How has being a part of such places contributed to your image of God and self?

3. If you're not currently part of a spiritual community, what would you list as the most important features for you when searching for one to join? If you are part of a community, what draws you back to gather with them? What do you hope could be different?

4. Think of a time when someone helped you interpret a faith experience. What did they help you realize about it that you might not have considered by yourself? Have you ever done the same for someone else? Is there an encounter you're currently wondering about where you might benefit from another's perspective?

Chapter 9

Responding to Grace

Years ago, I embarked on a group immersion trip to the Texas-Mexico border. It was led by Sister Margaret, a Catholic nun who'd made this trek many times and whose passion about the issues relevant to that area was clear over the few short days we spent together. During our brief stay, we toured one of the border villages, its dirt streets lined with makeshift houses constructed from wooden shipping pallets. We heard about labor practices by American companies that build maquiladora factories just over the border to escape U.S. regulations, complete with oppressively long hours and poor treatment of workers. We helped hang drywall in a building next to a Catholic mission that would serve as a food pantry. Everywhere I looked, I saw the desperate conditions of poverty that cause so many to attempt to flee to the United States.

One afternoon, my group attended a meeting of representatives from the factory workforce to hear about their situation and discuss their concerns. Our guide was an American advocate who worked closely with them on these issues. He served as our translator while prompting the workers to share not just with us but with one another the possible actions they could take toward improving their quality of life and work environment.

Near the end of this meeting, Sister Margaret shared with them parting words before we moved on to our next activity. As our guide translated, she encouraged them to press on in their struggle to make their voices heard and to promote their needs as best they could for themselves and their fellow workers. In closing, she said (paraphrased), "I believe that what you are doing is of God, and I pray that God will bless you in this important work."

I experienced a slight surprise when she said this. I was in a place in my own faith journey where considering the plight of factory workers on the U.S.-Mexico border to be "of God" was a strange concept to me. This strangeness was equal parts theological and cultural: in those days I believed that God's greatest concern was for personal salvation and the resistance to individual temptation and sin. I hadn't yet explored with any depth how God might also be concerned about systemic sin that demeans and dehumanizes some for others' benefit. This theological worldview was borne out of a comfortable middle-class existence that could afford to spend more time thinking about my own spirituality and less about how it could inspire me to care for others, much less those in the conditions that I saw during my trip.

As I have mentioned, spirituality is personal. We develop it for ourselves based on our experiences in prayer, study, and reflection in community. However, spirituality also has implications for how we view and interact with our surroundings. It is not meant to be compartmentalized on our plate, never to touch the other areas of our lives, but instead to saturate all of it. We may not tend to ponder the ways our family or career is "of God," let alone the critical issues of our day. Giving those matters their own box where we measure them using a different set of criteria may be far easier than applying those we use when engaging in spiritual practice.

On the contrary, contemplation moves us beyond our personal altars and prayer stations in order to face the world which God has created and loves. Contemplation leads to considering how each interaction that makes up our day, each location in which it happens, and each individual and societal issue that we encounter is "of God." We may ask: what does God have to say about this moment, and how might I respond to it faithfully? In an argument with my spouse, how is God holding both of us close? What might be happening with my visibly agitated co-worker that I may never know, and how might I reflect God's love to them? How is God concerned about each destructive story playing out in the news, and how do I need to move beyond snap judgments and partisan loyalty to share that concern?

Nurturing our spirituality is not meant to be a hobby apart from the rest of our lives, but instead the basis for our lives as a whole, alongside our physical and emotional needs. This nurturing begins with the transformation of the self, but moves outward toward the transformation of our larger world as we respond to God's presence.

The Possibility of Self

As I have explored, spirituality begins with considering our images of God and self, how the relationship between them functions in our lives, and how each evolves in light of new experiences. Spiritual direction invites us to ask these questions and encourages us to engage in prayerful practices that nurture this awareness. These practices may include forms of listening prayer such as meditation, which invites reflection on imagery related to general truths and how we react to that imagery. We may also engage in contemplation, which further personalizes our experience of God through intentionally imagining Biblical passages, giving close attention to our own emotional reaction to the events therein.

Practicing these forms of prayer over time causes a new sense of God and self to emerge within us. At some point, our prayerful consideration of suggested imagery begins to include who we are in God's world. We move from contemplating scripture to contemplating the interactions at our favorite coffeehouse, the water lapping at the edge of the lake where we spend summer weekends, the feel of a toddler's soft, warm feet against our cheek. All objects, people, and events invite contemplation of God's self-giving presence as we experience them.

As our contemplative awareness grows, we are invited to consider not only what is, but also what could be. God's activity in a given moment may be moving us toward a possibility not yet considered. We see this often in the prophets of the Hebrew scriptures. Called by God to deliver a message to the people of Israel or Judah, they were charged with a twofold task: first, to identify the divine undercurrent of the nation's life. Most often, this involved naming the people's neglect of something with which God had charged them, such as trusting God instead of making allegiances with others out of fear and desperation, or giving more attention to the poor and downtrodden instead of ignoring or exploiting their predicament in favor of one's own comfort.

In addition to this important calling, prophets were charged with delivering a message of what could be if people returned to faithful behavior. In Isaiah 58, for instance, the prophet shares vivid imagery of his people becoming like a lush garden watered by fresh abundant springs, where dry places yet again yield all manner of produce and former times of lavishness would be enjoyed once again by all. This possibility would come to pass if the people would turn their thoughts back to God's purposes for them to care for one another.

Spiritual direction doesn't necessarily turn us into prophets, but it does encourage us to identify the divine undercurrent of each moment, as well as the possibility in which we may participate when tuned into what God is doing. Not only is the present moment "of God," but we may consider how the next moment may be as well. And our own awareness and response may help such a moment come into bloom.

In his letter to the Romans, the Apostle Paul describes the process of cultivating this awareness and possibility within ourselves:

What then are we to say? Should we continue in sin in order that grace may abound? By no means! How can we who died to sin go on living in it? Do you not know that all of us who have been baptized into Christ Jesus were baptized into his death? Therefore we have been buried with him by baptism into death, so that, just as Christ was raised from the dead by the glory of the Father, so we too might walk in newness of life.

For if we have been united with him in a death like his, we will certainly be united with him in a resurrection like his. We know that our old self was crucified with him so that the body of sin might be destroyed, and we might no longer be enslaved to sin. For whoever has died is freed from sin. But if we have died with Christ, we believe that we will also live with him. We know that Christ, being raised from the dead, will never die again; death no longer has dominion over him. The death he died, he died to sin, once for all; but the life he lives, he lives to God. So you also must consider yourselves dead to sin and alive to God in Christ Jesus. (Romans 6:1–11 NRSV)

Having just described the free gift of love, forgiveness, and transformation that God gives to us in chapter 5, Paul turns his attention in chapter 6 to the nature of this gift and its capacity to change our view of the world. Much as he does in other letters, he first argues against abusing this gift: rather than serve as a license for behavior free of consequence or accountability, it opens up a new way of living.

Referencing the words used in baptism, which employed the language of dying to the old and being raised into the new, Paul writes, "Therefore we have been buried with him by baptism into death, so that, just as Christ was raised from the dead by the glory of the Father, so we too might walk in newness of life" (6:4). As stated during this sacrament, we have buried the ways of the past in order to embrace the new life that God's gift inspires. The old self is buried, and the new self that seeks and celebrates resurrection and renewal of creation—including the transformation of our false self to the true—takes its place.

Any spiritual director will be careful and quick to point out that such a transformation of consciousness doesn't take place overnight. Burying the false self and addressing habits, hang-ups, wrong turns, and mistakes that hinder us from being our true God-graced self takes time and effort. Healing the ways we have hurt or been hurt by others; transcending the scars of moments past in order to move toward who God wishes us to be may involve a long process of purposeful restoration.

Seeing how each moment is "of God" may be quite difficult, particularly those that keep us chained to comfortable prejudices, patterns, and self-involved attitudes. But the self-giving God of reckless forgiveness is persistent, and dedicated contemplation of this divine gift's unfailing presence allows us to see ourselves and each situation that we experience with new eyes.

Open Eyes, Open Hands

Regular observance of prayer and other spiritual practices, as well as routine meetings with a spiritual director, help cultivate a new awareness of God and self. This awareness radiates outward to affect those with whom we interact. Our sense of our relationship with God begins with an inward nurturing, but also influences our relationships with others, both loved ones and strangers alike.

Our inner consideration eventually affects outward action. We are invited to prayer; to lift up our joys, cares, anxieties, and very selves to God. We may do this through petitions of naming people and situations for which we are concerned. We may do this through listening forms of prayer such as meditation and contemplation in order to open ourselves to God's guidance. But discernment of God's presence and message also involves a tangible response. As we lift up a problem that we or another is facing, it may be through prayer that we discover that we are part of the solution, or at least can help bring greater comfort or assistance to ease the burden of another. I don't mean to say that prayer in itself cannot change a situation. Rather, we might be the ones that prayer changes in order to offer assistance.

In Matthew 6, part of what is typically called the Sermon on the Mount, Jesus gives several teachings on the spiritual practices of almsgiving, prayer, and fasting:

> *"Beware of practicing your piety before others in order to be seen by them; for then you have no reward from your Father in heaven.*
>
> *"So whenever you give alms, do not sound a trumpet before you, as the hypocrites do in the synagogues and in the streets, so that they may be praised by others. Truly I tell you, they have received their reward. But when you give alms do not let your left hand know what your right hand is doing, so that your alms may be done in secret; and your Father who sees in secret will reward you.*
>
> *"And whenever you pray, do not be like the hypocrites; for they love to stand and pray in the synagogues and at the street corners, so that they may be seen by others. Truly I tell you, they have received their reward. But whenever you pray, go into your room and shut the door and pray to your Father who is in secret; and your Father who sees in secret will reward you.*
>
> *"And whenever you fast, do not look dismal, like the hypocrites, for they disfigure their faces so as to show others that they are fasting. Truly I tell you, they have received their reward. But when you fast, put oil on your head and wash your face, so that your fasting may be seen not by others but by your Father who is in secret; and your Father who sees in secret will reward you."* (Matthew 6:1–6, 16–18 NRSV)

For each of the practices mentioned, Jesus advises against too public a display in order to win observers' affection. First, he says:

"whenever you give alms, do not sound a trumpet before you, as the hypocrites do in the synagogues and in the streets, so that they may be praised by others" (Matt. 6:2). Here Jesus engages in a little satirical hyperbole: there was no customary sounding of a trumpet during the offering in 1st Century places of worship. His point is that some liked to make a grand showing of their giving in order to receive admiration. Instead, Jesus says to make one's contributions in secret, "and your Father who sees in secret will reward you" (6:4).

Jesus follows a very similar formula for prayer and fasting. For prayer, he describes the hypocrites praying on street corners while instructing his audience to pray secretly to God in their rooms with the door shut, "and your Father who sees in secret will reward you" (6:5–6). And likewise with fasting: advice against looking dismal and despairing in hunger like the hypocrites. Instead of shuffling along giving a sour-faced performance, he says wash your face, stand up straight, and act as if nothing is happening, "and your Father who sees in secret will reward you" (6:16–18).

Why does Jesus teach about spiritual practices in this way? There are several possibilities. First, he gives a closer relationship with God as the reason for these practices. In all three, he names God as the only observer who matters. Almsgiving was and is a practice of sharing one's resources with others, but it is also a spiritual discipline that produces a more giving attitude and a greater awareness of what one has and may give away. Likewise, prayer and fasting open one's heart and mind to a deeper understanding of God's calling. Such disciplines are to draw a person closer to God.

Second, in all three teachings Jesus uses the term "hypocrites" for those who make big displays of their practice. In the modern use of this word, we tend to think of a hypocrite as someone who says one thing, but then does something entirely contrary. In Jesus' day, the term came from two Greek words meaning "judge" and "from behind." It most commonly referred to actors who judged who their characters were from behind masks. Such a person was playing or performing a role in public, pretending to be someone they weren't.[1] Jesus seemed to know that the false self can manifest in overtly religious ways. Perhaps we've found that by engaging in certain rituals, participating in a particular tradition, or professing certain beliefs has helped make us more lovable to family, friends, or the town in which we live. Or, conversely, we may engage in such practice or affiliation for fear of being shunned by such groups. So we perform our role, hoping to maintain approval as best we can. The mask of the false self that is painted with religious markings can be the most spiritually damaging.

Finally, does this secrecy of practice lead to anything? If, as Jesus says, we are to pray in secret, what sort of difference will it make for anyone besides ourselves? After all, the same person who offers this teaching also says to let one's light shine through good works, to love one's enemies, to reconcile with neighbors with whom there is a dispute, and to show forgiveness to others just as God has shown forgiveness. How might we resolve these teachings that seem to contradict each other?

Spiritual practices are some of the ways through which God transforms people. We observe them to draw into deeper relationship with God, allowing ourselves to become swept up in our increased sense of God's activity around us. Some may be inspired as a result of seeing us give alms, hearing us pray on a street corner, or seeing our faces pale with hunger as a result of fasting. Instead, these practices inspire the observer to see God in our enemies, in neighbors with whom we are arguing, and in those whom we are meant to forgive. In grateful response to the self-giving God who sees in secret, we serve as a result of what we have discerned in prayer. Such practices help us to see that there is a lot more in the world that is "of God" than we thought.

Directions on the Road

I pastor a church near Akron, Ohio. As a mid-sized city close to where many of the members of my congregation live, they tend to choose from among its hospitals and affiliates when they need to be treated for illness or injury. As such, I find myself making many trips into Akron every year to visit and pray with those recovering from various ailments. I have two main routes that I take into the city, depending on the hospital, each of which will get me to my destination in 15 or 20 minutes.

I can believe whatever I want about each of these routes. I can believe that one route is the better way than the other on a particular day. I can hold beliefs about the amount of time it will take me depending on traffic patterns at specific times of the day. I can believe that all of my fellow drivers should follow one way over another. But no matter what I believe about the best way to get to Akron, I'll never actually make it to Akron unless I actually follow the way I prefer. I need to take actual steps toward pursuing the way, such as getting in my car, making a definite decision about my route, pulling out of the church parking lot, and adhering to prescribed driving laws.

Spiritual direction involves the examination of beliefs. Meeting with a spiritual director will include an invitation to consider one's images of God and how God is in relationship with us. For Christians in particular, this may involve thinking about one's views on Jesus, the Holy Spirit, sin, the cross, resurrection, discipleship, grace, forgiveness, and a host of other theological topics as conceptualized by the Christian faith. Meeting with a spiritual director will help bring clarification of what one believes, free of judgment or manipulation.

But the spiritual journey is about more than belief. It is also about following a way; how one's beliefs about his or her relationship with God informs their interaction with the world. Our response to a God of reckless forgiveness and gracious imminence involves enacting forgiveness and graciousness toward others.

This sort of responsive transformation happens gradually, and is a topic with which a spiritual director will gladly help. Such transformation may involve goal-setting such as watching for examples of Jesus' call to love one's neighbor between meetings. This may involve processing a moment when it was especially hard to discern God's presence while dealing with a difficult person. It may involve talking through possibilities for how best to be Jesus' disciple in one's workplace. Between the conversation during meetings with one's director and the discernment that takes place during prayer, such changes will usually take place in small, intentional increments.

A woman with whom I was meeting for spiritual direction described an interaction she had with a rude customer. After noting that there would have been a time when she would have reacted to the man's behavior in a much harsher manner, she shared that this time around, she felt a presence, as if someone was watching her. Her awareness of God's closeness changed her perception of the encounter and her response to it. After weeks of our meeting together and her own prayer observances, she saw the way this ordinary handling of a difficult work situation was "of God," as well as the possibility of the future moment given her own participation in its divine undercurrent.

There are many steps between who and where we are today and where and who we could be in response to God's self-giving presence. Such steps are part of the way we are invited to follow. Spiritual direction helps us identify these steps according to our own experience and circumstances, each of which are "of God," no matter the specifics.

Questions for Reflection

1. How often would you say you allow your spirituality to influence decisions related to family, career, or other areas of your life? What might prevent you from considering how these are "of God?"

2. What experiences, wounds, or anxieties help keep your false self in place? What might need to be buried in order to live into new possibilities of God and self?

3. Consider Jesus' teachings about observing spiritual practices in secret. How do you think this applies to your own life? What attitudes or behaviors that you display when interacting with others would you hope a regular prayer practice could begin to transform?

4. What sort of way forward do you hope to follow regarding spiritual direction? What possibilities do you believe God is setting before you? How could you address this with someone else?

Chapter 10

Immersed in God's Presence

Every summer, my family takes a week's vacation to Florida. We go with my wife's side of the family to stay in a condo just a few hundred yards from the Atlantic Ocean. It's always an enjoyable week of relaxation, digging in the sand with our kids, and sightseeing in the area.

The main attraction for us is the ocean itself. I always look forward to hearing the sound of the waves crashing in the surf; that first glimpse of the sun reflecting off the water every morning. After everyone has woken, enjoyed a light breakfast, and applied sunscreen, we try to get down to the beach as early as we can before the heat of the day starts to assert itself.

When you are actually in the ocean, it becomes the only thing that matters. You have to be acutely aware of your surroundings. You have to anticipate when the next wave is about to wash under (or sometimes over) you. You have to be aware of your footing and depth. You have to be aware of the strength of the undertow and whether you're drifting too far from your preferred place in the water. You have to be aware of others around you and whether you might be encroaching in their space, or they in yours.

When you are immersed in the ocean, it determines your thoughts and behavior because it makes itself the primary concern in your consciousness. No matter what else you're doing, an awareness of what the water is doing influences all of it.

If fully considered and embraced, spirituality affects everything that you do. It is not meant to receive its own compartment and be displayed only when convenient. Instead, Christian spirituality cultivates an awareness that we are immersed in God's presence, and no matter the specifics, an attentive consciousness to that will influence the way we see and interact with God, ourselves, and the world. Spirituality is tending our capacity to be vigilant of this divine presence in and around us.

A Psalm of Awe

The writer of Psalm 111 names this vigilance in a slightly different way. This psalm is one of praise seemingly written from the viewpoint of an individual rather than on behalf of an entire people, although the first verse suggests a sense of community with others: "Praise the Lord! I will give thanks to the Lord with my whole heart, in the company of the upright, in the congregation" (Psalm 111:1). Many psalms that begin similarly or feature this general spirit of praise and thanksgiving.

After this introduction, the psalmist launches into the cause of his preliminary exclamation:

> *Great are the works of the Lord,*
> *studied by all who delight in them.*
> *Full of honor and majesty is his work,*
> *and his righteousness endures forever.*
> *He has gained renown by his wonderful deeds;*
> *the Lord is gracious and merciful.*
> *He provides food for those who fear him;*
> *he is ever mindful of his covenant.*
> *He has shown his people the power of his works,*
> *in giving them the heritage of the nations.*
> *The works of his hands are faithful and just;*
> *all his precepts are trustworthy.*
> *They are established forever and ever,*
> *to be performed with faithfulness and uprightness.*
> *He sent redemption to his people;*

> *he has commanded his covenant forever.*
> *Holy and awesome is his name.*
> *The fear of the Lord is the beginning of wisdom;*
> *all those who practice it have a good understanding.*
> *His praise endures forever.* (Psalm 111:2–10 NRSV)

God's "work" and "deeds," repeated over and over in this psalm, are the reasons for the psalmist's praise. Both are great, honorable, and majestic, and through them God has made God's name known.

Here the psalmist is describing both a past and a present reality. The reference to God's "wonderful deeds" echo past descriptions used in the foundational narrative for the Israelite people, particularly in Exodus 3:20 and 15:11. The description of God providing food could be an allusion to God providing manna and quail in the wilderness, and God remembering the covenant recalls God's decision to remain in relationship with the Israelites after the golden calf episode in Exodus 32.[1] The psalmist is remembering his nation's sacred history with fondness and thanksgiving, while also celebrating that this experience continues to be true for him personally, and for the congregation in which he sings.

The phrase "gracious and merciful" appears several other times in the Hebrew scriptures. The use of the phrase here once again recalls a story from the exodus narrative where God self-reveals and self-declares to Moses a series of promises and attributes, where these adjectives are prominent. In Exodus 34:6, God is described as "merciful and gracious, slow to anger, and abounding in steadfast love and faithfulness." Several other psalms of praise use variations on this phrase as well.

Psalm 111 is a psalm of celebration. It offers thanksgiving for God's wonderful deeds past and present, which reinforce an image of God who is gracious and merciful. Near the end of the psalm, however, the author uses another phrase which at first glance may seem to contradict this image: "The fear of the Lord is the beginning of wisdom; all those who practice it have a good understanding. His praise endures forever" (111:10).

The use of the word "fear" may at first suggest an image of God mentioned in chapter 2, which a man admitted to William Barry he hated: a threatening tyrant who waits and watches for human beings to mess up in order to render judgment and punishment. "Fear" most typically suggests being frightened or living in terror. Is this truly how a God described as gracious and merciful behaves, or what such a God demands from followers? Is this the same God of forgiveness and transformation that we find in Jesus? Perhaps there is another possibility.

While divine encounters by Biblical figures do often feature a reaction of terror and recoiling, this reaction is not caused by a threat or display of wrath on God's part so much as the spectacle of the moment and a realization of God's holy otherness. Yet God's grace and mercy makes it possible for the one experiencing God's presence to approach, and they do so in humble gratitude.[2]

Consider, for instance, the prophet's reaction to his vision in Isaiah 6:

> *In the year that King Uzziah died, I saw the Lord sitting on a throne, high and lofty; and the hem of his robe filled the temple. Seraphs were in attendance above him; each had six wings: with two they covered their faces, and with two they covered their feet, and with two they flew.*
>
> *And one called to another and said: "Holy, holy, holy is the LORD of hosts; the whole earth is full of his glory."*
>
> *The pivots on the thresholds shook at the voices of those who called, and the house filled with smoke. And I said: "Woe is me! I am lost, for I am a man of unclean lips, and I live among a people of unclean lips; yet my eyes have seen the King, the LORD of hosts!"*

> *Then one of the seraphs flew to me, holding a live coal that had been taken from the altar with a pair of tongs. The seraph touched my mouth with it and said: "Now that this has touched your lips, your guilt has departed and your sin is blotted out." Then I heard the voice of the Lord saying, "Whom shall I send, and who will go for us?" And I said, "Here am I; send me!"* (Isaiah 6:1–8 NRSV)

Upon encountering seraphs flying in the great temple, with their earth-shaking proclamations of God's holiness, Isaiah laments his perceived unworthiness for this moment; his being unfit to be in God's presence, let alone act as God's mouthpiece for the people. And yet, after a burning coal touches his lips, he is called into service, an act of mercy by a God of grace. Isaiah's experience embodies the type of fear that the psalmist has in mind: one less of terror and more of reverence and thankfulness for what he has received from God through no act of his own.

Thus what typically is deemed a psalm of praise could be termed a psalm of awe. The psalmist expresses a reverent awareness of what God has done historically for his people, but also for God's ongoing works of grace and mercy. God was not like this only once upon a time, but is still actively present in this same way for the writer and the congregation of which he is a part. God has created and creates, has provided and provides, has shown and still shows grace.

But it is not enough for the psalmist to be aware of who God is. What really matters, he writes, is to live in active consciousness of God's identity and presence and to allow for that to affect one's actions and decisions. An active awe and reverence of a gracious and merciful God who has done and is still doing wonderful works, is the beginning of wisdom. "The fear of the Lord" is a view of the world accounting for God's place and one's own, where no corner of one's life goes untouched.[3]

Psalm 111 presents an image of God who exhibits grace and mercy as foundational traits, reflected by acts of creation, redemption, and provision both past and present. These acts are not for their own sake, but to inspire a life of awe and reverence in which grace and mercy are paid forward to others. As discussed in a previous chapter, Jesus would later embody and reveal this same image.

Fear, Reverence, and Disorder

The psalmist uses the word "fear" to mean reverence. Those things to which we devote the most energy and attention are the things that we revere. They are what inform our decision-making and how we spend our time. We might not always be conscious of what affects us in this way. Through honest self-reflection and feedback from others, we may be able to discern this for ourselves.

The Franciscan friar and spiritual writer Richard Rohr observes that we are all part of certain structural boxes that influence our lives. We are most beholden to what helps us maintain a sense of security and status. We may be most reverent toward our careers, mortgages, schedules, or systems from which we derive privilege, even if at another's expense.[4]

It might be quite fitting, then, that many Biblical translations use the word "fear," because what we revere most tend to be what we are most fearful of losing. This will, in turn, inspire in us a sense of self-preservation, where whatever it takes to maintain the lifestyle to which we are accustomed and from which we most benefit will take precedence over everything else.

Ignatius of Loyola referred to this tendency as having "disordered attachments." When we become preoccupied with our own jealousies, greed, grudges, comfort, need for control, and perfectionism, we put them at the center of our lives rather than God. We give reverence and power to them and make choices out of anxiety over their potential loss; a felt need to preserve what we have at all costs.[5]

Our need for control is among the most dangerous and leads to many of these attachments. When aspects of our lives seem to be spinning away from our grasp, the details too many to pin down, we may turn to indulgences that help us feel stable, even if they add to the chaos more than remove it. This may include alcohol, drugs, sex, food, work, or emotional relationships. We believe we are engaging in these on our terms, when in reality we become dependent on them in unhealthy ways. Our disordered attachment controls us, rather than the other way around.

In my first few years in pastoral ministry, I made what I did at the church my first concern. I agonized over each week's sermon, I would drop everything to visit someone in the hospital even on days off, and I attended every meeting. When a congregant died while I was on vacation—this happened often, which was uncanny for a church of that size—I would rush back to help the family prepare the funeral. On one occasion when this happened, my wife remarked, "I'll never understand this part of what you do."

As the years progressed, I was able to see the full spirit of her comment's meaning. Unbeknownst to me, I had made my career the center of my life at my family's expense. I look back and wince at all the moments during my earliest ministry years when not being able to accomplish a task on my preferred timetable affected my mood and behavior toward others. At the time, I couldn't see the ways I sacrificed other parts of my life. After all, this was not just a job but a calling, as we in ministry are fond of saying.

In retrospect, I can name the factors that played a role in my disordered attachment. First, I had a felt need to prove myself: I was a young seminary graduate, newly ordained, privy to rumblings among my congregation that due to my age and experience, I might not be as attentive to certain ministry tasks as some would prefer. Second, based on a bad experience that my father had in his final settled pastorate, I had a fear of losing what I had. Every misstep in those early years caused a rush of anxiety about the damage it might cause in my relationship with the congregation.

Due to these factors, I set the church—of all things—in a place of reverence. My concerns about job security, status, and maintaining a sense of perfection and effectiveness were my biggest motivations. It wasn't until later, after more than one conversation with family and colleagues, that I could see the ways this all affected my temperament and relationships with loved ones. I needed to step back and examine what I revered, and shift my priorities accordingly.

When we are in this sort of place spiritually, we lose sight not just of God's presence, but of the type of God who is present. In giving reverence to those things that we believe provide us with safety and honor, we implicitly make them our source of identity and meaning.

Immersion, Wisdom, and Awe

While the writer of Psalm 111 doesn't reflect on preoccupation with disordered attachments, he does imply his awareness of the ongoing temptation. After all, he writes that the "fear of the Lord," placing God in that proper place of reverence and awe, is the beginning of wisdom. When we are attentive to God's presence and activity, when we receive and live into God's transformative forgiveness, that is the beginning of wisdom. When we are in awe of the ways God is moving around us, and make space both to discern it more readily and respond to it more faithfully, that is the beginning of wisdom.

The opposite, what the psalmist may call unwise and Ignatius does call disordered attachment, is elevating other objectives to that place instead. When we do so, we become less aware of God's presence in our surroundings. We don't realize where we are drifting or when we're out of our depth. We become blind to the ways we may be encroaching on other people to get what we want or what we think we need. We create disorder for ourselves and often for those we love.

Ignatius had a similar idea. The culmination of his *Spiritual Exercises,* known as the Contemplation to Obtain Love, is his "sending forth" of sorts to the one completing the practice. In the second prelude, he guides the exercitant to ask for what he or she wants:

> Here, it will be to ask for interior knowledge of all the good I have received, so that acknowledging this with gratitude, I may be able to love and serve his Divine Majesty in everything.[6]

In Ignatius' view, humanity's main purpose is to revere and serve God in all things. This reverence comes not from fear of God's consequences, but thankfulness for what God first shares with us. For both the psalmist and Ignatius, God's many gifts revealed through creation inspire gratitude, love, and service. Realizing what God has given inspires change; a reorientation toward a God continually sharing in the raw material of our lives. This awareness is the beginning of spiritual growth.[7]

When I realized that I had made the church an inordinate priority above other parts of my life, a new realization of my family's love for me was what most inspired me to change. This realization involved some frank conversation, but even that emanated from a place of love; a treasuring of my time and attention, which they both desired and needed. This love, the gifts that they wanted to share with me, most influenced my desire for transformation.

Have you ever stopped to consider the people who love you? Have you ever reflected on the unconditional gifts of time, care, and sacrifice that you receive from others, because they take joy in your thriving and happiness? They do this because they want to be in relationship with you; to gift and be gifted by who you are. A deeper realization of my family's love for me helped inspire a greater reverence for the attachments that matter, and put those that cause disorder in proper perspective.

Pausing for such reflection can be awe-inspiring. You may come away with new understanding of the one who loves you, as well as feel gratitude for what they see in you. This is the way of spiritual life and practice: to inspire awe for the divine love and presence in which we are immersed, and by that same love begin to live in reverence and wisdom.

This includes seeing the face of God in the people we encounter in coffeehouses, and sweeping the floor with Brother Lawrence. It includes contemplating God's presence during a long road trip, and searching for new expressions of God's light in times of darkness and desolation. It includes remembering that an ever-present God of reckless forgiveness is always communicating with flawed and anxious people, including ourselves.

All of creation, Ignatius notes, may point this out to us and is useful to this end. Our participation in that reality makes praise, reverence, and service possible.[8] In scripture, art, music, and poetry; in families and communities we trust; in daily tasks and special celebrations, God shares in and communicates through it all.

When we become increasingly aware of our immersion in the raw stuff of God's creative activity; our floating in the waves of God's movement, it invites our reverent response. We are called away from our disordered attachments, our destructive images of God and self, into a new way of engaging the world. A proper life of reverence, the psalmist suggests, is centered on God's awe-inspiring and wondrous deeds. Our thankful response is the beginning of wisdom; the continuation of our spiritual journey.

Questions for Reflection

1. Can you think of a time when you were inspired by the love of another? How did it affect you? In what ways did you change?

2. What "disordered attachments" are you dealing with? In what ways could you begin to address them with yourself? With others?

3. What would you say you revere most in your life? Could any of what you list be considered a disordered attachment? In what ways might what you list reflect the love of God?

4. Having reached this last chapter, how would you now define "spirituality?" How has your definition changed since the beginning of this book? Where might you turn to continue your spiritual exploration?

Afterword

Looking Back and Moving Forward

At this point, a natural question to ask might be, "What next?" Having been introduced to concepts like meditation, contemplation, discernment in community, and spiritual direction, where do you go from here? What next steps might you wish to take to continue this journey of discovery and new awareness?

My answer to that is twofold: *look back, and move forward.*

First, *look back*. Throughout this book, I have encouraged you to look back and identify important points along the road that have helped shape you into who you are and who you understand God to be. When doing this, you might consider treasured relationships, educational experiences, and spiritual influences such as faith communities or individuals who somehow radiated the divine to you. You might name defining moments where you felt at peace within yourself, or desolate times that have both left scars and inspired personal growth.

Look back upon these landmarks on the road, and give thanks. Each of them have shaped you; have taught you something about the world, about yourself, and about your relationship with God and others for which you might not have had the words at the time. You may still be searching for adequate avenues through which to process them.

In his foreword, John Dorhauer's recollection of key experiences and communities that have shaped his spirituality caused me to think about my own. My road began and has traveled through the theology, history, and relational understanding of my own denomination, the United Church of Christ. However, that road at different points has made brief detours through evangelical, United

Methodist, Christian Church (Disciples of Christ), and Catholic belief systems and practices that have had an impact on how I relate to God and others. Not all of these experiences have been positive, but they have all left a lasting impression. I look back at them and, with enough time, distance, and reflection, give thanks for them.

So first, look back. Like those disciples walking to Emmaus, you may be able to name points along the way when your heart was burning even if you couldn't say why.

After looking back, *move forward*. I have described spiritual direction throughout this book, and you may now be wondering how or where to find a spiritual director to continue walking with you. A few possibilities exist for this that will depend on your location, context, and needs.

First, you may wish to consult the website of Spiritual Directors International, a global directory of spiritual directors with a "Seek and Find" option for registered directors near you. A second option is to contact local retreat centers, as they may work regularly with spiritual directors and could help you connect. A third option might be searching for spiritual direction certification programs close to you, as they no doubt keep up to date records of people whom they have trained.

In addition to finding people, you may also wish to continue reading. Many other authors, scholars, and spiritual guides have contributed wonderful writing on the topics of prayer and spiritual direction. If you wish to continue exploring theology and practice related to these topics, here are a few other resources I would recommend.

Driskill, Joseph D. *Protestant Spiritual Exercises: Theology, History, and Practice*. Harrisburg, PA: Morehouse Publishing, 1999. Beginning with the acknowledgment that many spiritual practices are rooted in Catholic faith and tradition, Driskill explains how non-Catholic believers may find them meaningful as well. Major themes in this work include an introduction to several spiritual disciplines and guidelines for using them.

McColman, Carl. *Answering the Contemplative Call: First Steps on the Mystical Path*. Charlottesville: Hampton Roads Publishing Company, 2013. McColman provides an excellent overview of what one needs to consider when taking a more intentional approach to spiritual practice. Suggestions include how to become comfortable with silence, finding companions (such as a spiritual director), and a list of writings by other mystics that may aid your journey.

McLaren, Brian. *Finding Our Way Again: The Return of the Ancient Practices*. Nashville: Thomas Nelson Publishers, 2008. I've long found McLaren to be a thoughtful and inviting writer, and this work serves as the introduction to a series of books titled *The Ancient Practices Series*, edited by Phyllis Tickle. Other works in the series explore practices such as keeping Sabbath, fasting, and praying The Divine Hours. McLaren first explains how observing such practices may enrich one's faith.

Merton, Thomas. *New Seeds of Contemplation*. New York: New Directions, 1962. Considered to be one of Merton's best-known and beloved books, *New Seeds of Contemplation* is a collection of brief reflections on contemplative prayer; what it is and isn't. He covers topics such as being willing to be alone, recognizing God in all experiences, and allowing contemplation to affect how one interacts with others.

Neeld, Elizabeth Harper. *A Sacred Primer: The Essential Guide to Quiet Time and Prayer*. Los Angeles: Renaissance Books, 1999. I hold this resource close because it helped open the doors to my own spiritual journey during that introductory seminary class. Neeld's book is divided into three parts: laying the theological foundation for why one might wish to pursue spiritual practice, preparing oneself for observance, and exploration of several basic aspects of practice such as seeking quiet, listening, and how to pray.

Nouwen, Henri. *Spiritual Direction: Wisdom for the Long Walk of Faith*. New York: HarperCollins Publishers, 2006. A beloved writer of many spiritual classics, Nouwen here provides insight specifically regarding the benefits of receiving spiritual direction. Each chapter begins with a presumed question one may ask about this practice, which he then explores with insight and grace. Any of Nouwen's books will be spiritually enriching, but this will help explain spiritual direction specifically.

Tetlow, Joseph. *Making Choices in Christ: The Foundations of Ignatian Spirituality*. Chicago: Loyola Press, 2008. A longtime scholar of Ignatius of Loyola and of the Spiritual Exercises, Joseph Tetlow is a must-read for delving deeper into the Ignatian tradition. This work features brief, thoughtful reflections on the themes of the Exercises and would be a good companion to spiritual direction that is based on them.

Wherever your journey has led thus far, and wherever it may yet lead, I wish you blessings on the way. And whether in the breaking of bread or while in line for coffee, may the gift of God's gracious self-giving presence bring consolation.

Notes

Notes to Chapter 1

1. Henri Nouwen, *Spiritual Direction* (New York: HarperCollins, 2006), xiii.
2. Henri Nouwen, *Life of the Beloved* (New York: Crossroad, 1992), 133.

Notes to Chapter 2

1. Howard Rice & James Huffstulter, *Reformed Worship* (Louisville: Westminster John Knox, 2001), 83–91.
2. Joseph Driskill, *Protestant Spiritual Exercises* (Harrisburg, PA: Morehouse, 1999), xii.
3. Mark Oppenheimer, "Examining the Growth of the Spiritual but Not Religious," *The New York Times* (July 18, 2014), online, accessed March 20, 2015. 4. R. Alan Culpepper, "The Gospel of Luke," in *The New Interpreter's Bible, Volume IX*, ed. Leander E. Keck et al. (Nashville: Abingdon, 1995), 480.
5. Karl Rahner. "Nature and Grace," from *Theological Investigations 4* (Limerick: Mary Immaculate College, 2004), 809.
6. Rahner, "Nature and Grace," 818–19.
7. John P. Galvin, "The Invitation of Grace," from *A World of Grace*, ed. Leo J. O'Donovan (Washington, DC: Georgetown UP, 1995), 66.

Notes to Chapter 3

1. Alister McGrath, *Christian Theology: An Introduction* (Oxford: Wiley-Blackwell, 2010),188.
2. Harvey D. Egan, "Christian Apophatic and Kataphatic Mysticisms," *Theological Studies* 39.3 (September, 1978): 403.
3. Ibid., 422.
4. William Barry, *Finding God in All Things* (Notre Dame: Ave Maria, 2008), 23.
5. This term may be spelled "kataphatic" or "cataphatic," depending on the source or audience. I use kataphatic simply because the majority of my references chose this spelling.
6. Egan, "403.

7. Ibid., 424.
8. McGrath, 188.
9. Kevin O'Brien, *The Ignatian Adventure* (Chicago: Loyola, 2011), 55.
10. Karl Rahner, "On the Theology of the Incarnation," in *Theological Investigations 4* (Limerick: Mary Immaculate College, 2004), 772.
11. R. Alan Culpepper, "The Gospel of Luke," in *The New Interpreter's Bible, Volume IX,* ed. Leander E. Keck et al. (Nashville, Abingdon, 1995), 169–70.
12. Ibid., 170.
13. Fred Craddock. *Luke* (Louisville: John Knox, 1990),106.
14. Barry, Finding God in All Things, 51.
15. William Barry. *Letting God Come Close* (Chicago: Loyola, 2001), 176.
16. Marilyn Sunderman, "Grace and Lived Christianity in the Theology of Karl Rahner and Leonardo Boff," *International Journal of Humanities & Social Science* 1.8 (July, 2011): 278.

Notes to Chapter 4

1. Karl Rahner. "Theology and Anthropology," from *Theological Investigations 9* (Limerick: Mary Immaculate College, 2004), 1859–60.
2. Anne Carr, "Starting with the Human," from *A World of Grace,* ed. Leo J. O'Donovan (Washington, D.C.: Georgetown UP, 1995), 17.
3. Jaco Hamman, *Becoming a Pastor* (Cleveland: Pilgrim, 2007), 25–6.
4. Each of these tools grant insight to how one relates to oneself and others. The Myers-Briggs and Enneagram tests use extensive self-assessment questions resulting in the classification of the individual into a general personality type. The Johari Window adds an element of soliciting opinions from others to help the subject understand how one presents him or herself to the world. To find out more about these tools, visit the following links:
www.myersbriggs.org
www.enneagraminstitute.com
www.usgs.gov/humancapital/documents/JohariWindow.pdf
5. Gerd Theissen and Annette Merz, *The Historical Jesus* (Minneapolis: Fortress, 1998), 140.
6. Teresa of Avila, *Interior Castle* (Mineola, NY: Dover, 2007), 15–6.
7. Ibid., 17.

Notes to Chapter 5

1. Michael Ivens, *Understanding the Spiritual Exercises* (Herefordshire: Gracewing, 2008), 46.

2. Richard Foster, *Celebration of Discipline* (San Francisco: Harper San Francisco, 1998), 20.

3. Thomas Merton, *Contemplative Prayer* (New York: Image, 2014), 10.

4. Ivens, 46.

5. Ibid., 90.

6. Thomas Merton, *New Seeds of Contemplation* (New York: New Directions, 1962), 1.

7. Stephen Patterson, *The God of Jesus* (Harrisburg, PA: Trinity International, 1998), 120.

8. Kevin O'Brien, *The Ignatian Adventure* (Chicago: Loyola, 2011),141.

9. William Barry, *Letting God Come Close* (Chicago: Loyola 2001),104.

Notes to Chapter 6

1. Thomas Merton. *New Seeds of Contemplation* (New York: New Directions, 1962), 5.

2. John Galvin, "The Invitation of Grace," from *A World of Grace: An Introduction to the Themes and Foundations of Karl Rahner's Theology,* ed. Leo J. O'Donovan, (Washington, D.C.: Georgetown UP, 1995), 65.

3. Brother Lawrence, *The Practice of the Presence of God* (Grand Rapids: Spire, 1967), 30.

4. Ibid., 44.

5. Galvin, 67.

Notes to Chapter 7

1. Karl Rahner, "On the Theology of the Incarnation," in *Theological Investigations 4* (Limerick: Mary Immaculate College, 2004), 778.

2. Marilyn Sunderman, "Grace and Lived Christianity in the Theology of Karl Rahner and Leonardo Boff," *International Journal of Humanities & Social Science* 1:8 (July, 2011): 280.

3. Michael Ivens, *Understanding the Spiritual Exercises* (Herefordshire: Gracewing, 2008), 216.

4. Kevin O'Brien, *The Ignatian Adventure* (Chicago: Loyola, 2011), 165–6.
5. Ibid., 182.
6. Walter Brueggemann, *The Message of the Psalms* (Minneapolis: Augsburg, 1984), 52.
7. James Mays, *Psalms* (Louisville: John Knox, 1994), 106.

Notes to Chapter 8

1. Raymond Collins. "Church, Idea of the," in *The New Interpreter's Dictionary of the Bible,* ed. Katharine Doob Sakenfeld et al. (Nashville: Abingdon, 2007), 1:644.
2. John Calvin, *The Institutes of Christian Religion,* ed. Tony Lane and Hilary Osborne (Grand Rapids: Baker, 1987), 234.
3. Michael Fahey, "On Being Christian—Together," from *A World of Grace,* ed. Leo J. O'Donovan (Washington, D.C.: Georgetown UP, 1995), 128–9.
4. Michael Ivens, *Understanding the Spiritual Exercises* (Herefordshire: Gracewing, 2008),14.

Notes to Chapter 9

1. Emerson Powery. "Hypocrisy, Hypocrite," from *The New Interpreter's Dictionary of the Bible,* ed. Katherine Doob Sakenfeld et al. (Nashville: Abingdon, 2007), 2:925.

Notes to Chapter 10

1. J. Clinton McCann, Jr., "Psalms," in *The New Interpreter's Bible Volume IV,* ed. Leander E. Keck et al. (Nashville: Abingdon, 1996). 1133.
2. Harold Washington, "Fear," in *The New Interpreter's Dictionary of the Bible,* ed. Katharine Doob Sakenfeld et al. (Nashville: Abingdon, 2007), 2:442.
3. Christine Roy Yoder. "Psalm 111, Exegetical Perspective," in *Feasting on the Word, Year B,* vol. 1, ed. David L. Bartlett and Barbara Brown Taylor (Louisville: Westminster John Knox, 2008), 301.
4. Richard Rohr, *Eager to Love* (Cincinnati: Franciscan Media, 2014), 35.
5. Kevin O'Brien, *The Ignatian Adventure* (Chicago: Loyola, 2011), 57–8.

6. Michael Ivens, *Understanding the Spiritual Exercises* (Herefordshire: Gracewing, 2008), 172.

7. William Barry, *Finding God in All Things* (Notre Dame: Ave Maria, 2008),176.

8. Ivens, 30.

Bibliography

Barry, William. *Finding God in All Things: A Companion to the Spiritual Exercises of St. Ignatius.* Notre Dame: Ave Maria Press, 2008.

———. *Letting God Come Close: An Approach to the Ignatian Spiritual Exercises.* Chicago: Loyola Press, 2001.

Brother Lawrence. *The Practice of the Presence of God with Spiritual Maxims.* Grand Rapids: Spire Books, 1967.

Brueggemann, Walter. *The Message of the Psalms: A Theological Commentary.* Minneapolis: Augsburg, 1984.

Calvin, John. *The Institutes of Christian Religion.* ed. Tony Lane and Hilary Osborne. Grand Rapids: Baker Book House, 1987.

Carr, Anne. "Starting With the Human." *A World of Grace: An Introduction to the Themes and Foundations of Karl Rahner's Theology.* Ed. Leo J. O'Donovan. Washington, D.C.: Georgetown UP, 1995. 17–30.

Collins, Raymond. "Idea of the Church." *The New Interpreter's Dictionary of the Bible.* Vol. 1. Ed. Katharine Doob Sakenfeld et al. Nashville: Abingdon Press, 2007. 643–655.

Craddock, Fred. *Luke.* Louisville: John Knox Press, 1990.

Culpepper, R. "The Gospel of Luke." *The New Interpreter's Bible.* Vol. 9. Ed. Leander E. Keck et al. Nashville, Abingdon Press, 1995, p. 3–490.

Driskill, Joseph. *Protestant Spiritual Exercises: Theology, History, and Practice.* Harrisburg, PA: Morehouse Publishing, 1999.

Egan, Harvey. "Christian Apophatic and Kataphatic Mysticisms." *Theological Studies* 39.3 (September, 1978): 399–426.

Fahey, Michael. "On Being Christian—Together." *A World of Grace: An Introduction to the Themes and Foundations of Karl Rahner's Theology.* Ed. Leo J. O'Donovan. Washington, D.C.: Georgetown UP, 1995. 120–137.

Foster, Richard. *Celebration of Discipline: The Path to Spiritual Growth.* San Francisco: HarperSanFrancisco, 1998.

Galvin, John. "The Invitation of Grace." *A World of Grace: An Introduction to the Themes and Foundations of Karl Rahner's Theology.* Ed. Leo J. O'Donovan. Washington, D.C.: Georgetown UP, 1995. 64–75.

Hamman, Jaco. *Becoming a Pastor: Forming Self and Soul for Ministry.* Cleveland: Pilgrim Press, 2007.

Ivens, Michael. *Understanding the Spiritual Exercises.* Herefordshire: Gracewing, 2008.

Mays, James. *Psalms.* Louisville: John Knox Press, 1994.

McCann, J. "The Book of Psalms." *The New Interpreter's Bible.* Vol. 4. Ed. Leander E. Keck et al. Nashville: Abingdon Press, 1996. 641–1280.

McGrath, Alister. *Christian Theology: An Introduction,* 5th Edition. Oxford: Wiley-Blackwell, 2010.

Merton, Thomas. *Contemplative Prayer,* 2014 Image ed. New York: Image Books, 2014.

———. *New Seeds of Contemplation.* New York: New Directions, 1962.

Nouwen, Henri. *Life of the Beloved: Spiritual Living in a Secular World.* New York: Crossroad, 1992.

———. *Spiritual Direction: Wisdom for the Long Walk of Faith.* New York: HarperCollins, 2006.

O'Brien, Kevin. *The Ignatian Adventure: Experiencing the Spiritual Exercises of Saint Ignatius in Daily LIfe.* Chicago: Loyola Press, 2011.

Oppenheimer, Mark. "Examining the Growth of the Spiritual but Not Religious." *New York Times* (July 18, 2014), online, accessed March 20, 2015.

Patterson, Stephen. *The God of Jesus: The Historical Jesus and the Search for Meaning.* Harrisburg, PA: Trinity Press International, 1998.

Powery, Emerson. "Hypocrisy, Hypocrite." *The New Interpreter's Dictionary of the Bible.* Vol. 2. Ed. Katherine Doob Sakenfeld et al. Nashville: Abingdon Press, 2007. 925–926.

Rahner, Karl. "Nature and Grace," *Theological Investigations 4,* Electronic Centenary ed. Limerick: Mary Immaculate College, 2004. 810–824.

———. "On the Theology of the Incarnation." *Theological Investigations 4,* Electronic Centenary ed. Limerick: Mary Immaculate College, 2004. 773–782.

———. "Theology and Anthropology," from *Theological Investigations 9,* Electronic Centenary ed. Limerick: Mary Immaculate College, 2004. 1870–1881.

Rice, Howard and James Huffstulter. *Reformed Worship.* Louisville: Westminster John Knox Press, 2001.

Rohr, Richard. *Eager to Love: The Alternative Way of Francis of Assisi.* Cincinnati: Franciscan Media, 2014.

Sunderman, Marilyn. "Grace and Lived Christianity in the Theology of Karl Rahner and Leonardo Boff." *International Journal of Humanities & Social Science* 1.8 (July, 2011): 278–284.

Teresa of Avila. *Interior Castle.* Mineola, NY: Dover Publications, 2007.

Theissen, Gerd and Annette Merz. *The Historical Jesus: A Comprehensive Guide.* Minneapolis: Fortress Press, 1998.

Washington, Harold. "Fear," in *The New Interpreter's Dictionary of the Bible.* Vol. 2. Ed. Katharine Doob Sakenfeld et al. Nashville: Abingdon Press, 2007, p. 438–442.

Yoder, Christine. "Psalm 111, Exegetical Perspective." *Feasting on the Word, Year B, Volume 1.* Ed. David Bartlett and Barbara Brown Taylor. Louisville: Westminster John Knox Press, 2008. 296–301.

Index

apophatic tradition, 27–28, 37

baptism, 19–20, 85, 99, 112–113
Barry, William, 28, 33–34, 66, 124
Brother Lawrence, 74, 78, 130

Calvin, John, 13, 99
church
  as community, 4, 98–103, 107
  as institution, 7, 77, 107, 127–129
  practices of, 12–16, 19–21, 74
communion, 18–20, 74, 78
contemplation, xi–xii, 55, 57–58, 66, 67–68, 76–78, 110, 111, 114, 133, 135
consolation, spiritual, 92–93, 94, 136

desolation, spiritual, 85–87, 91–93, 94
Driskill, Joseph, 134

ekklesia, 99

false self, 44–51, 68, 72–73, 83, 105, 113–114, 117, 120

God, attributes of
  forgiveness, 32–34, 36, 49, 68, 82, 83, 103, 105, 113–114, 117–119, 124, 128, 130
  grace, 19–21, 23, 34, 41, 46–47, 51, 52, 64–65, 74, 76–77, 83–84, 86, 103, 107, 125–126
  imminence, 36, 68, 119
  transformation, 34–37, 45, 68, 72, 82, 83, 103, 111, 113–114, 117, 119, 120, 124, 128–129

Gregory of Nyssa, 27

Hamman, Jaco, 44

Ignatius of Loyola, iv, 3, 11, 49, 54, 56–57, 63–64, 67, 85, 126, 128–130, 136
  Spiritual Exercises of, 3, 11, 50, 56, 59, 63, 106, 129
Ivens, Michael, 56

kataphatic tradition, 28–30, 37

McColman, Carl, 135
McLaren, Brian, 135
meditation, xiii, 2, 8, 11, 55–58, 66, 67, 92, 111, 114, 133
Merton, Thomas, 56, 58, 67, 135
Michigan, 95–97, 101–102

Neeld, Elizabeth Harper, 135
Nouwen, Henri, 5–6, 136

O'Brien, Kevin, 29

petition prayer, 5, 54–55, 87, 114
pneuma, 46

Rahner, Karl, 19–20, 30, 34, 41, 68, 84, 102
ruach, 46

sacraments/sacramental, 19–20, 22, 24, 76, 99–100, 113
"spiritual but not religious," 14–15, 24, 98

spiritual direction
  definition, 2–8, 9, 53, 136
  practice of, xii, 11, 40–42, 45, 49, 51, 53, 63–64, 76–77, 93,

    98, 106, 111–112, 118–120,
    133–134

Teresa of Avila, 50
Tetlow, Joseph, 136
true self, 44–51, 52

United Church of Christ/UCC, xi,
    12–13, 79–80, 100, 133

Made in the USA
Columbia, SC
25 August 2018